CRAZY PATCHWORK

Janet Haigh

CB

CONTEMPORARY BOOKS

Published in the United States in 1998 by The Quilt Digest Press
A division of NTC/Contemporary Publishing Group, Inc.
4255 West Touhy Avenue, Lincolnwood (Chicago),
Illinois 60646-1975, U.S.A.

International Standard Book Number: 0–8442–2664–5

Library of Congress Cataloging-in-Publication Data
Haigh, Janet.
Crazy patchwork/Janet Haigh.
p. cm.
Includes index.
ISBN 0–8442–2664–5
1. Patchwork—Patterns. 2. Machine quilting—Patterns.
3. Embroidery. Machine—Patterns. 4. Quilted goods. I. Title.
TT835.H26 1998
746.46'041—dc21   98–7661 CIP

A BERRY BOOK
Conceived, edited, and designed by Susan Berry for Collins & Brown Limited
London House Great Eastern Wharf Parkgate Road London SW11 4NQ

Editor • Sally Harding
Design and Art Direction • Debbie Mole

Managing Art Editor • Kevin Williams
Executive Editor • Ginny Surtees

Photography • John Heseltine
Illustrations • David Ashby and Kate Simunek

Reproduction by Hong Kong Graphic & Printing Ltd.
Printed in the United States.

CONTENTS

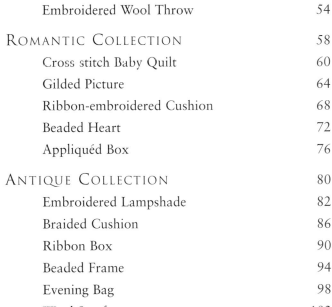

INTRODUCTION

T H I S   B O O K *is for everyone who collects fabrics, ribbons, buttons, and beads, for everyone who can't resist rescuing the tattered remnants of once glorious embroideries, the unraveling beaded bag, the torn lace collar, the linen handkerchiefs with embroidery in one corner and rust stains in the other, the ripped silk headscarves, the tarnished gold braids—in fact, anything irresistible and cheap enough to buy and that makes you think, "I'll do something with this some day..."*

I HAVE A collection such as this; it ranges from exquisite hand embroidered silk ribbons bought in the Portobello Road flea market in the 1960's to my father's old-fashioned neckties, from well-worn and ripped Chinese skirts to children's tartan kilts bought in a thrift shop. I have lived with, and added to, this collection for years, occasionally using tiny pieces for my embroidered pictures, but more often pinning them to my studio wall as inspiration for designing fabric collections or just to brighten dull days.

If you're like I am, you will say to yourself everytime you add to your semi-precious collection, "I'll save that and do something with it, sometime." Well, now is the sometime and here is the something—crazy patchwork.

Crazy patchwork uses irregular scraps of beautiful fabrics. And all kinds of textiles—velvets, silks, and tartans—are used together, for unlike conventional patchworks, which rely on repeating patterns or contrasts in tones for their effect, crazy patchwork relies on the variety and quality of its basic materials.

Crazy-patch fabrics serve to create a sumptuous ground for a mixture of simple embroidery techniques, that used separately or together give these unique patchworks their highly decorative appearance. With its embroidered seams and motifs, its words, messages, and embellishments, crazy patchwork provides the perfect destination for all your favorite materials.

Though the end result is sumptuous, the fabrics need not be valuable or costly. Think of the beauty of clean, freshly laundered cottons, ginghams, linens, *broderie anglaise*—all easily obtained and reasonably priced, particularly if bought secondhand. And what about those treasured denim jeans, so old and faded that they can no longer be decently worn? Cut them up, embroider your memories onto the scraps, and crazy patchwork them together to make your own very personal crazy heirloom.

I first made a crazy patchwork as a way of solving a problem posed by a commissioned embroidered portrait. The commissioning couple had five children but did not want them all portrayed as figures in the portrait; however, they did want some reference to them all. I had, at the time, a diary featuring antique American quilts that included a crazy quilt, and it occurred to me that this technique was an excellent device for incorporating a lot of visual information. Each child could have his or her own patched square containing personal symbols that would give the viewer a variety of facts about that person. I extended the idea to give the parents, the house, and the garden their own squares as well. When completed, all the crazy-patch squares were used to frame the simple embroidered portrait of the couple and the family dog (see page 8).

Thus initially intrigued by crazy quilts, I started to research and study everything I could find out about them

and discovered a wealth of embroidery and image-making techniques within their history. As well as all types of embroidery, I found painting and writing on fabric, which included signatures, messages, and headlines from contemporary newspapers. I also found stitched into the quilts such things as silk patches printed with cigarette advertisements, patches that were slipped into cigarette packs and probably designed especially to be incorporated in patchworks. All in all the crazy quilts turned out to be a

fascinating compendium of the times that they were made in.

The collaging of all these different design elements, seemed so modern in its concept that it was fascinating to discover that the majority of these quilts were made in the late nineteenth century. The first antique quilts I studied were either the American ones I found in books, or British ones I could visit in museums; they had much in common. The fabrics were costly and beautiful velvets, silks, and brocades, or bright and jewel-like cottons and wools.

Later I discovered the simpler versions made from household linens, ticking, ginghams, denims, and decorated with everyday objects interpreted in back-stitch; these now look so fashionable at the end of the twentieth century when the preference seems to be for simple, unpretentious styling.

Crazy quilts were a fashion themselves in the United States and Europe in the late nineteenth century. This seems to have coincided in the United States with the Centennial Exposition held in Philadelphia in 1876. In Britain during this time crazy patchwork was the perfect textile embodiment of the Victorian taste for exuberant decoration.

The general opinion is that the discovery of Japanese design gave rise to this vogue for crazy quilts that

BELOW *This portrait, commissioned in the late 1980's, was the author's first foray into designing crazy patchwork.*

swept the United States and Europe. Introduced first into the West in the 1860's, Japanese arts and crafts revolutionized the artistic and fashionable taste of the era. The Japanese pavillion at the Philadelphia show was the most popular. And I can imagine that, seen for the first time, the asymmetrical, seemingly haphazard qualities of Japanese imagery might have been appeared "crazy." However, the usual view is that the cracked and crazed patterns found in many Japanese textiles and ceramics look like the random patches in crazy patchwork. Japanese motifs abound in the early quilts—fans, cranes, and all kinds of other Oriental imagery.

This needlecraft became so popular in the United States that merchants packaged fabrics cut into crazy shapes with diagrams of motifs ready to copy and stitch onto the fabric, and advertised them in the popular press. The

fashion was not for quilts but for smaller items, such as cushion covers, throws, tea cozies, and occasionally dressing gowns. The richness of detail and the precious nature of the cloth made the items difficult to launder (not such a problem now that we have dry cleaning), so the quilts that were made were kept for best.

However, what really fascinates me about the old crazy quilts is that people often used them as I have—as a record or memento of someone. Sometimes they were made from a dead child's clothes, with names and dates lovingly embroidered into the patches. More often they were made as a present or as a record of a community celebrating some special occasion; you don't really need a great deal of skill to make a crazy quilt, unlike a conventional quilt, so everyone could contribute.

Many of the celebratory quilts were packed with splendid handwritten messages and autographs. It was these features that recently provided both a solution and an inspiration for me when I was commissioned to make two large wall hangings for the Roy Castle Foundation in Liverpool. My working brief was to record and celebrate the charity's success in raising the money to build an international scientific research center dedicated to the knowledge and eventual eradication of lung cancer. The funding was provided by patients and their families and a vast network of people worldwide.

I had to include many different pieces of information, both visual and narrative, in the commission. The fundraising activities ranged from marathon runs and mountain climbs, to coffee mornings, national popular entertainers pledging box office takings of shows, to golf competitions.

Dozens of people had to be depicted: from the local consultant surgeon, who conceived the idea, to Nelson Mandela, who had received a deputation

LEFT *One of the two hangings designed by the author for the Roy Castle Foundation. It was commissioned to record and celebrate the charity's success at raising funds for a research center for lung cancer.*

BELOW *This detail from the Liverpool Hangings shows the influence of traditional crazy patchwork and the incorporation of modern-day logos and portraits.*

from the charity on its well-publicized world tour. I had to assimilate all this imagery into two cohesive embroidered hangings while collecting all the data piecemeal, and I had a six month deadline! Then I remembered crazy quilts.

The traditions and the variety of techniques encapsulated in crazy patchwork give the inventive embroiderer a great deal of inspiration. The following pages are full of ideas for making many different types of designs: some are elegant, some useful, some are included just because they arc inspirational. I hope that they will inspire you to create fabrics that appear beautiful to you, for what you choose to add to your patchworks will be personal to you, or the people that you make them for.

To help you get started, the first chapter explains all sorts of things that you will want to know, like . . . How do I choose my fabrics? Which fabrics work well together? Which colors do I use? How do I get my materials to work like those in the pictures? What can I do with just a small piece of patchwork? Can I do this quickly? All will be revealed.

As well as the most useful and interesting embroidery techniques and stitches that will enable you to make your own quilts, the book includes simple step-by-step instructions for making smaller items that will incite you to happily start cutting into your precious collection of fabric scraps and trims. If you haven't got a collection, this is the book to get you started!

MAKING THE PATCHWORK

This chapter explains all you need to know to make crazy patchwork—from how to collect fabric scraps, to how to join patches and add your favorite embellishments.

T HE PAGES THAT FOLLOW are meant to guide you through the simple but captivating processes involved in making pieces of crazy patchwork from start to finish, and from the simplest designs to the most elaborate and ornate.

The adventure begins, as with all scrap quilts, with building up a collection of fabric remnants. Unlike conventional patchwork, however, crazy patchwork allows for the use of an unusually wide and exciting range of fabric textures, weaves, and weights. Advice is given on how to find your crazy-patch scraps and what to choose, how to organize the scraps into compatible groups, and most importantly how to create a color scheme for your patchwork.

Easier to piece together than conventional patchwork, crazy patches are simply stitched at random to a foundation fabric and the seams decorated. Several piecing techniques are included in this chapter, along with a range of seam and patch embellishment methods that make crazy patchwork both unique and magical.

THE EMBROIDERER'S ALPHABET

O R S T U
V W X Y Z

For embroidering, use the cotton, flax and silk articles, mark D.M.C.

The Bare Necessities

The odyssey of crazy patchwork begins with gathering together the bare necessities

of the craft, which include fabric scraps, foundation fabric, embellishment trims and

threads, and simple sewing and embroidery tools.

THOSE WHO SEW AND embroider for pleasure will already have at hand most of the tools, equipment, and threads needed to try out crazy patchwork. Putting together the remaining ingredients—fabric scraps and trims—could easily be considered the most enjoyable part of the craft. It will give you the excuse to start collecting all those stunning textiles, ribbons, braids, buttons, and beads that catch your eye, or to add to the collection you already have. You can buy as little as ¼yd (25cm) of fabric or ½yd (50cm) of braid at a time, and antique scraps can never be too small.

FABRICS AND TRIMS

TRADITIONALLY the fabrics used for patchwork have always been recycled, and those used for crazy patchwork are no exception. What makes crazy patchwork different is that all types and textures of fabrics can be used in combination because the patches are virtually "appliquéd" to a foundation fabric rather than seamed together. This fabric diversity contributes to the appealing richness of pattern, texture, and detail in crazy patchwork.

So where do all these fabrics come from? I have collected mine from thrift shops, rummage sales, and flea markets, and friends have given me precious scraps—too good to throw away, not good enough to sell. I have found all types of remnants in large stores and specialty fabric shops.

The fabrics that I collect fall basically into weaves, glitz, prints, checks and stripes, accessories, lace, and embroideries. Weaves include damasks, brocades, tweeds, tartans, and paisleys. Glitz is composed of metallics, lurex, brocades, and velvets. Prints include cottons, wools, silks, and are mostly flowered, some geometric. The checks and stripes incorporate tickings, ginghams, and madras weaves. Laces are grouped with *broderie anglaise*, net, and see-through fabrics. Accessories I collect are ties, handkerchiefs, and scarves.

The last category includes any embroidery I can find— old Chinese robes, European folk costume, Eastern handmade bodices, machine-stitched art deco blouses. Although all old and unwearable, they have really beautiful bits that will transform the other fabrics in a crazy patchwork into something very special.

LEFT *Shown in a rainbow of colors, here are some of the materials that can be used to trim and decorate your crazy patchwork. As well as, ribbons and braids of all types, your crazy-patch trim collection can include beads, shells, embroidered cutouts, charms, buttons, and even feathers! Embroidery threads that come in handy are cotton floss and pearl cotton, crewel and tapestry wools, metallics, twisted silks, embroidery ribbon, and special machine embroidery threads.*

ABOVE *Here is a varied selection of fabrics from my collection. They are loosely grouped according to type and this is how I keep my fabrics in my studio—in separate categories in large cardboard boxes, so that when designing I can easily pull out a "woven" fabrics box or rummage through a "glitz" box. You need to prepare secondhand scraps before you are ready to use them, unpicking seams or cutting away unusable parts, and saving interesting trims. If necessary, most fabrics can be safely washed in hand-hot water with a mild liquid soap. I seldom launder the exotics, such as fragile silks and colored embroideries, but only use them for pieces that will get little wear; dry cleaning fluids or sprays can be used with care.*

SORTING FABRICS AND TRIMS INTO COMPATIBLE GROUPS

YOU WON'T NEED AS LARGE a collection or as many types of fabric groups and trims as I have shown to get started on crazy patchwork. To begin with, just collect a pile of scraps that you like. Then get used to putting together successful patchworks by sorting your scraps into the compatible groups or "stories" that follow my three collections.

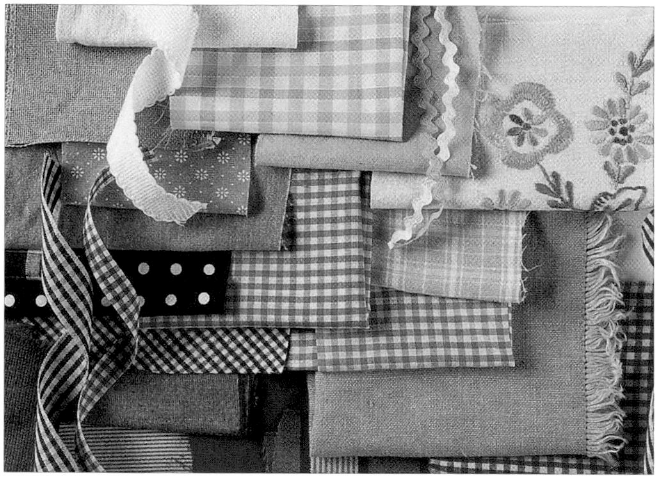

LEFT *These are the types of medium-weight fabrics and simple trims used for the crazy-patchwork projects in the Country Collection chapter (see pages 36–57). The look the collection aims for requires clean, fresh colors and natural fabrics. Think of ginghams, denim, chambray, ticking, woven and printed checks and stripes, dots, crisp linens, and plain household cottons—all fabrics that can be easily laundered. This type of fabric grouping looks especially appealing decorated with simple details such as figurative line embroidery, plain and check ribbons, and rickrack. Simple secondhand embroideries can be added sparingly as special highlights.*

For the novice patchworker, nervous about color and pattern, this design story is a good place to start.

RIGHT *This softer grouping of fabrics is the one used for the projects in the Romantic Collection chapter (see pages 58–79). Made up of light to medium-weight fabrics, it includes pretty small-scale floral, paisley, and plaid cotton prints in pastel shades, plain and printed silks, and* broderie anglaise. *Added for embellishment are antique scraps, such as old-fashioned tray cloths, lazy-daisied and appliquéd, fine lace, silk and rayon head scarves, and precious handkerchiefs. Ruched, ruffled, plaid, and machine- and hand-embroidered silk and rayon ribbons fit comfortably into the grouping.*

This design story is suited to those who enjoy working cross-stitch embroidery on evenweave aida and ribbon embroidery over patch seams.

LEFT *This is the grouping of fabrics and trims that is more usually associated with traditional crazy quilts. It includes a selection of scraps used for the projects in the Antique Collection chapter (see pages 80–105). These fabrics are heavier and more textured than those in the other two stories. They are the types of fabrics associated with evening or winter wear, and upholstery or curtains, and include brocades, velvets, and fine plain, paisley, and tartan wools, all in jewel brights or sedate and somber shades.*

Luxurious touches are incorporated in the form of machine-embroidered ribbons, antique hand embroidery, metallic fabrics and braids, velvet ribbons, and heavy laces—bond the rich finer lace to taffeta or lurex backings to make them weightier. This combination can't fail to please traditionalists.

EQUIPMENT AND OTHER MATERIALS

LEFT *The tools and equipment used for making crazy patchwork are mostly those used for basic sewing and simple embroidery. And not all crazy patchwork requires embroidery, since it can be embellished with ribbons, braids, and buttons just as successfully. If you are making your first crazy patchwork, just gather together the tools and equipment you have at hand and only purchase any really essential missing components. You can always slowly build up your supplies later.*

BE SURE TO TRY TO organize all the tools and equipment for making crazy patchwork before beginning. It is frustrating to have to stop the flow of enthusiasm once you have started arranging your patches and trims, just to find a simple tool. You will need general sewing equipment, embroidery tools, the appropriate foundation fabric, and batting if you are making a quilt. Specific materials and any special tools or ingredients—such as a latch or crochet hook for making fringe, metal leaf for gilded motifs, felt for making a stuffed heart—are listed with the projects.

Sewing equipment

Essential basic sewing equipment includes pins, a tape measure and ruler, needles for basting, a thimble, a seam ripper (for mistakes!), a drafting triangle (for marking square corners), and a water soluble marker pen. Also needed are dedicated paper scissors and fabric shears, and most importantly a pair of small scissors with sharp points—I keep mine on a long ribbon around my neck so that I don't loose them among the fabrics.

Contrasting basting threads are needed for basting patches in place, and invisible monofilament thread for machine zigzag-stitching patches, braids, and ribbons.

Having a sewing machine will speed up the crazy patchwork process, but it isn't a must, especially if you are making any of the small items in the book. If you do have a sewing machine, you will need a zigzag foot in order to machine zigzag patches together or for simple machine embroidery. And a jeans needle will come in handy for making bold decorative stitching with thick threads. Special embroidery attachments are optional extras.

Embroidery and appliqué materials

An embroidery hoop is essential for both appliqué and embroidery. Transferring equipment might also be called for—a pencil, tracing or tissue paper, dressmaker's carbon paper, and a water soluble pen. Graph paper and colored pencils are useful for charting cross-stitch designs.

You will also need crewel needles for embroidery, beading needles for bead embroidery, and chenilles for thicker threads and ribbon embroidery. For working cross-stitch on evenweave aida fabric or aida bands, a blunt-ended tapestry needle is required, while a pointed needle is used for working cross-stitch over waste canvas on non-evenweaves.

The only special material needed for appliqué is fusible bonding web, which is an adhesive that can be ironed onto the back of the motifs to stick them onto the ground fabric.

Foundation fabrics and batting

The best foundation fabrics for crazy patchwork are a plain fully shrunk cotton fabric or fusible woven interfacing. Whichever you choose, make sure it is firmly woven to give the patchwork a solid grounding and pale in color so that it will not show through lighter patch fabrics.

Batting is only necessary for making quilts. There are a range of synthetic and natural fiber battings to choose from, so you can choose one that suits your purposes. A lightweight natural cotton batting is ideal for baby quilts.

PATCH COLOR SCHEMES

You don't have to understand complicated color theory to choose the color schemes

for your patchworks; in fact, you can just imitate those given with the projects. But here are a few

tips for those who want to start grasping the basics of designing with colors.

WHEN DESIGNING a patchwork, the first thing I do is sort my fabrics into a color scheme. Many books, that I have read on crazy patchwork, suggest that you can put any fabrics together as and when they come to you, in a piecemeal fashion. Well, you can, but I wouldn't advise it unless you have a wealth of beautiful, flawless fabrics to choose from and an innate, highly developed sense of color.

My advice to you is to first experiment with color and try to understand some of the basics of color coordination.

Begin by arranging all your scraps into groups to form a rainbow as explained below. Then try making light, medium, and dark color schemes, schemes with varying tones, and a scheme based on a multicolored fabric. Lastly, experiment with how seam decoration effects a color scheme.

SORTINGS FABRICS INTO COLOR GROUPS

START COLOR experiments by arranging your fabrics into groups to form a rainbow of six colors: reds, oranges, yellows, greens, blues, and purples. First, sort all the plain colors into these six groups, then sort the individual color groups into tones—darks, mediums, and lights. Lay them in a circle to form a color wheel, or in a line to form a rainbow. It is now easier to see where the multicolored fabrics belong. Place the fabric where you feel that its dominant color belongs, then move away from it. Is it too light, too dark, too red, too blue? Move it around until it is in the right place.

RIGHT *Once the colors are arranged in a rainbow and in tones, you can freely choose from the separate color piles to try out the combinations suggested on pages 17 and 18.*

MAKING LIGHT COLOR SCHEMES

WHEN YOU begin making crazy patchworks, try to use colors from all six of the groups in the rainbow: reds, oranges, yellows, greens, blues, and purples. Many of the patchworks in the book employ this system. However, a good tip, especially for beginners, is to use only the fabrics with the same tonal intensity, that is all darks together, all mediums, or all lights. And stick to the same family of textures and weights in each scheme, lightweight fabrics that are lightly textured, heavy weights in heavy textures, and so on.

This grouping shows scraps from all six colors of the rainbow in light tones, or tints. The fabrics are all fairly light in weight and have very subtle textures.

MAKING MEDIUM COLOR SCHEMES

THIS SCHEME uses the same color principle as the light color scheme shown above: it combines colors from all six groups—reds, oranges, yellows, greens, blues, and purples. The fabrics are all compatible in weight, since they are all light to medium weight. This weight group encourages marginally more obvious and subtly coarser textures. You will notice how the selection of more plaids gives the combination a very different atmosphere from the light color scheme above, which is softened by a predominance of floral prints.

Try a medium-tone color scheme with lightweight florals, and light colors with medium-weight plaids to test the different effects that you can create.

MAKING DARK COLOR SCHEMES

AGAIN ALL SIX colors of the rainbow are represented in this dark color scheme. The fabrics are medium to heavy in weight, and the textures more obvious than those in the two schemes above. If you want to add a lightweight fabric to a grouping such as this, because the color is just right for the combination, don't despair; you can bond two fabrics together with fusible bonding web, or back the fabric with a fusible interfacing.

This scheme shows clearly how making a light, medium, or dark color scheme does not mean that the entire combination need be all light or all dark. Flashes of lights may appear comfortably in predominantly dark patterns or miniscule flashes of darks in light prints, and so forth.

MAKING A COLOR SCHEME WITH NEIGHBORING COLOR GROUPS

IF YOU DON'T HAVE THE FULL rainbow of colors in your collection, or your preferred color scheme is for something simpler than the six-color light, medium, or dark schemes on the previous page, you can limit the number of colors you use. To get fabrics that will successfully blend together, choose a few colors that are next to one another in the rainbow, for instance yellows, greens, and blues together, or reds, oranges, and yellows together, or reds, purples,

and blues together. You can usually use the whole range of tones when working with this system, that is lights, darks, and medium shades along with all the in-between shades.

But I sometimes find that when using deep, strong tones and very pale tones together, it can look as if the color has run in the wash—before I have even washed the patchwork! So I tend to change tones gently by placing darks next to mediums, mediums next to lights, and so on.

FRESH COLORS *Yellows, greens, and blues together create a fresh look. I tend not to use any black in light color schemes like this one, unless I am using it in a classic combination such as black and white, or black and cream.*

WARM COLORS *A red, orange, and yellow scheme looks warm and sunny. To knock back a white ground that makes a cream one look dirty or a color that is too bright for its companions, I sometimes carefully tea-dye the scraps.*

SUMPTUOUS COLORS *Reds, purples, and blues together look sumptuous. Black can be used in dark color schemes such as this. It can really make brights zing. Adding solid black with a pattern containing black makes it easier to use.*

TAKING A COLOR SCHEME FROM A MULTICOLORED FABRIC

THE SIMPLEST WAY to get a compatible group of colors together is to choose one multicolored stripe, check, or patterned scrap that you really love. Then match the colors in this fabric to some embroidery threads (as I have done here) or even some colored pencils. Match only the predominant colors—five or six are plenty. Take these threads to your piles of fabrics and choose a selection of scraps, both patterned and plain to match them. This technique simplifies the process of picking out the colors, since it is difficult to differentiate the colors correctly within a patterned design. Of course, now you also have the perfect harmonizing threads to embroider your crazy patchwork with!

RIGHT *This color scheme is based on the lovely paisley print at the center of the group. The five spools of embroidery threads that match the print have been used to select the other scraps.*

ADDING SEAM DECORATION TO A COLOR SCHEME

COVERING CRAZY-PATCHWORK seams with embroidery gives extra opportunity for introducing more color into your composition, or for balancing the color scheme by careful use of the chosen threads. Depending on the type of thread used, you can vary the overall look of the same crazy patchwork, as you can see by looking at the identical designs pictured below. Threads are not the only decorations you can use to introduce color; ribbons, braids, and beads can really change not just the color but the texture and the whole atmosphere of the patchwork.

Adding contrasting embroidery to the patches gives a design balance by evenly dispersing the various colors. But the quickest way to disperse colors is to machine stitch ribbons and braids over the seams. I took only fifteen minutes to add the ribbon and braid decoration to the piece shown below and forty minutes each for the embroideries.

TONING EMBROIDERY *Using toning or matching embroidery threads on the patches creates a subtle embellishment and emphasizes the individual patterns and textures of the fabrics.*

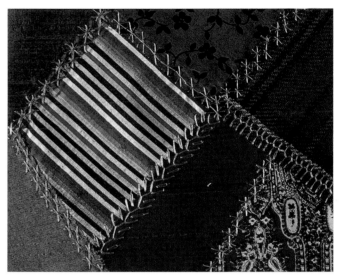

GOLD METALLIC EMBROIDERY *Metallic threads can look surprisingly subtle, yet not dull. I use bronzes and pewters on dark schemes and reserve bright metallics for lighter tints.*

BRAIDS AND RIBBONS *For a really rich and decorative fabric, adding trims like these is both simple and quick. Imagine how ornate this would look if I had hand embroidered the braids.*

CONTRASTING EMBROIDERY *I feel that using contrasting threads on the patches gives a better color balance. It also makes the stitches more prominent, creating a richer overall texture.*

CRAZY-PATCH PIECING

Unlike conventional patchwork, crazy patchwork is pieced together onto a backing or foundation fabric. This means that the piecing does not have to be so precise, and the patches can be secured with machine or hand stitches, or even simply bonded in place.

TRADITIONAL CRAZY quilts were made in various ways. Sometimes they were made in one large piece, the scraps just sewn on until the foundation fabric was covered. The more usual and convenient way was to make many large blocks, usually square; these blocks were then either embroidered together edge-to-edge or separated by plain strips of extra fabric, called sashing.

For most of the designs in the book, I have just made one small piece of patchwork. But each of these designs could be extended in the traditional way as the baby quilt has been with its sashing of aida bands (see pages 60–63). If it was to be used as a throw or quilt, a crazy patchwork was often finished with a crocheted or fringed edging.

Crazy quilts were seldom padded and quilted with stitches in the conventional way, since intricate stitching would have been lost amongst all the surface embroidery. Instead they were tied together at various points with threads or ribbons. Sometimes more decorative embellishments were used— buttons, beads, anything that took the maker's fancy.

MAKING A CRAZY-PATCH SQUARE

THERE ARE several ways to join your crazy patches to the foundation fabric. They can be pinned, basted, then machine zigzagged in place; they can be bonded to a fusible interfacing; they can be pinned, basted, then machine embroidered; or they can be pinned and hand embroidered. These specific stitching techniques are explained in detail on pages 22 and 23 (along with bead-pinned and lapped-seam patch techniques that are worked without a foundation fabric). Whichever technique you decide to use

to join your crazy patches to the foundation, read this sequence of steps first to gain an understanding of basics of crazy patchwork construction.

The crazy patchwork process is really quite simple and much easier and quicker than conventional patchwork. Don't worry about being too precise with patch cutting or positioning, since the random quality is part of the charm of the design. Make a few squares, trying out various color schemes. You can always use them later in a quilt!

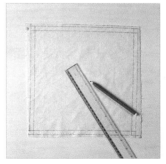

1 *Begin by preparing the foundation fabric (see page 15). Using a water soluble pen and a ruler, mark the finished size of the crazy patchwork block on the cotton foundation fabric. Then mark a second outline ³⁄4in (2cm) outside the first for the seam allowance.*

2 *Make a final decision about which patches you are going to use, and press any that are wrinkled. Cut a few roughly and randomly shaped patches. (Any embroidery or appliqué on individual patches should be worked before the scraps are joined to the foundation.)*

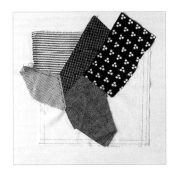

3 Select your first patch and place it on the foundation; it is usually easiest to start in a corner of the block and add the patches outward from there. Trim the piece to fit roughly into the corner, ensuring that it overlaps the seam allowance. The patch doesn't have to be cut exactly, the patch edges around the block will be trimmed later if they extend past the foundation edge. Pin the patch in place, but do not baste as the next patches will be basted on top.

4 Place the second patch next to the first patch, trimming the edges if necessary and overlapping the raw edges by about 1/4in (6mm). Pin, then baste the second patch, stitching through the two patches and the foundation. Then pin on the third patch, again overlapping the previous patch. Continue adding patches in this way. (Note that it isn't always necessary for a patch to overlap the preceding patch; it can also underlap, depending on how the patches fit together.)

5 After basting on about three patches, start securing the patches with machine stitches. Thread the machine and the bobbin with invisible monofilament thread and set it for a medium zigzag—not too wide and not too close (test on a piece of fabric first to check the tension). Use a medium-sized needle that is able to pierce three or four layers of fabric. Stitch along the basted edges, positioning the zigzag to cover the raw edge. Then continue basting on patches.

6 Continue filling the block, cutting patches in random sizes and shapes. Fill fanning out from the first corner toward the opposite one, or just let it grow naturally; there are no hard and fast rules. Make sure that the patterns are shown off to their best advantage, tilting any linear designs at angles to each other. Also, try to sprinkle the various colors across the block so that the same or very similar patches do not touch. Remove the basting as the zigzagging is worked.

7 Continue basting and zigzagging, filling the square as desired. Be sure to trim off any bulky edges on patches, such as French seams on shirt scraps, before adding the next overlapping patch. At the final corner, trim the final patch into shape and baste it in place.

8 Zigzag the final patch in place and remove any remaining basting threads. The final block will have a random appearance but with the various colors and fabrics spread around the square and not all bunched up in one corner. Press the block on the wrong side.

9 Before the patchwork is used to make something, the edge should be trimmed. The stitching might have caused the piece to shrink slightly. If you want to make it to an exact size, you should redraw the original shape on the back using a ruler and a water soluble pen.

10 Following the outline on the back, trim the edge parallel to it leaving the required seam allowance. After it is trimmed, the block is ready for the seam decoration. The seam decoration—embroidery or ribbons and braids—will cover the patch joins.

BONDED PIECING

TRADITIONALLY, crazy patches were placed together and pinned onto the backing, leaving the raw edges on the surface. Embroidery stitches secured the joins and hid the raw edges. These crazy quilts did not wear well. I have updated this method by using iron-on interfacing (or fusible web) to secure the patches before embroidering. This is strong enough for items that receive little wear, such as lampshades. For a more hardwearing fabric, the bonding can be used merely as a basting substitute prior to zigzagging.

LEFT When working bonded piecing, follow the piecing instructions on pages 20 and 21, but instead of using a plain cotton backing use a fusible woven interfacing; this eliminates the need for pinning and basting. Before bonding each patch, trim the underlapped edge to a neat line as it will show through as a ridge when the join is pressed. Using a piece of brown paper to cover the glue on the fusible interfacing if necessary, press each patch in place as it is trimmed and laid in position. Add seam decoration when the block is complete (see page 24).

MACHINE-STITCHED PIECING

IF A PATCHWORK needs to be very hardwearing, I machine zigzag the over-lapped raw edges using an invisible thread. This seaming technique can either be worked after the patches have been pinned and basted to a plain cotton foundation as shown on pages 20 and 21, or after they have been bonded to a fusible founda-tion as shown above. I prefer the bonding technique because it is faster, but a fusible interfacing is not always a strong enough foundation for items that will be frequently laundered.

Machine zigzagging over raw fabric edges with mono-filament thread is virtually invisible. Monofilament thread comes in a dark and

a light tone, and you should use the tone that suits your overall color scheme. Seam decoration will further obscure the zigzagging and the addition of braids or ribbons over the joins will competely cover them.

The other machine tech-nique shown here, lapped seaming, requires no foun-dation. With careful choice of stitches and fabrics, you can make a fully reversible fabric using lapped seams.

LAPPED SEAMING *To work lapped seaming, first baste the patches together to form the crazy-patch block, trim-ming them to fit each other and overlapping them by about 1/4in to 3/8in (6mm to 1cm). Then machine zigzag all the raw edges on one side using invisible thread. Next, turn the piece over, and zigzag the raw edges on the reverse side (see oval inset). Embroidery stitches can be neatly worked on the right side to cover the joins.*

MACHINE ZIGZAGGING *First pin and baste the crazy patches onto a strong cotton foundation fabric or bond them onto a fusible woven interfacing. The patches should overlap by about 1/4in (6mm). Zigzag over the raw edges as explained in Step 5 on page 21. Press the completed piece. (Since the pinned and basted patches are pressed before being laid on the foundation, there is no need to press each seam as it is worked.)*

MACHINE-EMBROIDERED PIECING

IF YOU HAVE A SEWING machine that has the facility to stitch embroidery, you can secure crazy patches and decorate the seams at the same time with a variety of machine satin stitches. Many machines do really fancy stitches. The ones that create the heavier, thicker patterns are the ones that I think work best. Crazy patchwork is not a delicate medium, and some of the prettier, finer stitches just look weak and weedy on top of a myriad of patterned fabrics.

1 *Following your sewing machine manual, test the available stitches. Try them using a large-eyed jeans needle, and a thick thread, such as glossy twisted silk or even metallic threads.*

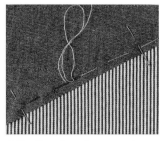

2 *Overlap the raw edges, and pin and baste the crazy patches in place as instructed in the steps on pages 20 and 21, or bond them in place as explained on the opposite page.*

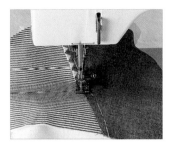

3 *Work machine embroidery over the raw edges and through the patches and the foundation fabric. Stop and start at patch corners, changing the stitch on each side of each patch for variety.*

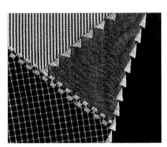

4 *Remove the basting threads. If your machine doesn't do fancy stitches, you can machine zigzag the joins; this can be just as decorative if you use a large stitch and a thick embroidery thread.*

DECORATIVE HAND PIECING

CRAZY QUILTS made in the nineteenth century were, of course, pieced onto the foundation fabric without the use of a bonding or a sewing machine. The patches were pinned and/or basted onto the foundation and then the raw edges were embroidered in place. Double and triple feather stitch were especially popular because they covered and secured the edges so well and were highly decorative. I usually like to use hand embroidery as a solely decorative technique rather than a securing technique, and machine zigzag raw edges in place first (see pages 24 and 25). But on small items embroidery can be worked quite quickly.

For items that will be washed frequently, it is probably best to fold under the raw edges on the patches while piecing them.

Beaded pinning is not a traditional decorative hand piecing technique for crazy patchwork, since it requires a tightly stuffed surface to hold the pins in position. Pinned and beaded heart cushions are, however, a traditional keepsake, invented when pins were valuable and given as presents to babies and sweethearts. I enjoy making them as presents for friends, decorated and dedicated for all types of celebrations. The pins should be rustproof, gold or silver lace pins are good for bead pinning.

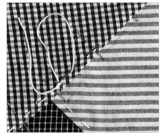

HAND EMBROIDERY *To secure patches with hand embroidery, pin the patches in place on the foundation fabric as explained on pages 20 and 21, but fold under the overlapping patch edges as you are piecing. Then using a bold embroidery thread, such as pearl cotton, work the chosen embroidery stitch along the joins removing the pins as you go. Use any stitch you desire (see pages 108–113); even simple running stitch can look effective.*

BEADED PINNING *Follow the instructions for making a stuffed heart on page 123 and for beading a heart on pages 52–53 and 74–75. Pins, decorated with beads and sequins, are used to secure the patches to the heart. If the beads are spaced apart, the patch edges should be folded under. Raw patch edges can be completely covered if sequins are placed under the beads and they are placed close together along the patch edges.*

SEAM EMBELLISHMENTS

After crazy patchwork has been pieced onto its foundation, it is time to decorate

the seams with hand or machine embroidery, or ribbons and braids. For further flourishes, you can

embellish patch corners with tassels, buttons, or ribbon rosettes.

MAKING CRAZY PATCHWORK is like making a collage. The beauty of it is that it can't go hopelessly wrong. If something looks inappropriate, I just stitch something else on top. Adding seam decoration gives you just such an opportunity. By choosing the right type and color of the embroidery threads or stunning ribbons and braids, you can transform a prepared crazy patchwork into something much more appealing and something that looks quite different from the bare patchwork (see page 19). No wonder elaborate seam decoration is one of the treasured hallmarks of traditional crazy quilts.

Although hand and machine embroidery can be used as a securing technique during piecing, I find that either bonding the patches in place or zigzagging them with invisible thread first, or both, suits just about every type of seam decoration and helps to create a very secure patchwork. It also leaves you free to complete the piecing before deciding on the type of seam decoration you will be adding to the patchwork.

Pages 24–27 provide a visual overview of a wide range of seam decorations, covering various types of embroidery threads, ribbon and bead embroidery, machine embroidery, and ribbon and braid seam embellishments. There is also a selection of patch corner decorations, used to cover awkward collisions of seam braids or seam embroidery.

The examples shown are all taken from the design projects in the collections or the alternative patchworks given with these designs. You will find more ideas for decorations by leafing through the book.

HAND EMBROIDERY OVER SEAMS

INSTRUCTIONS for stitches that can be used to decorate crazy-patchwork seams are given on pages 108–113. Traditionally the most common stitches used were double and triple feather stitch, herringbone stitch, and ornate combination stitches. I believe that the crucial component to successful hand-embroidered seams is the using the right type of thread and choosing colors that stand out at a distance. Cotton, silk, metallic, and wool threads, as well as silk embroidery ribbon can all be used. The important thing is to use thick enough threads (or enough strands) to give the embroidery audacity.

COTTON-THREAD (OR SILK) EMBROIDERY *Shiny, twisted pearl cotton was worked in herringbone stitch over the seams on this patchwork. I use thick, shiny twisted silk threads as often as possible, but pearl cotton can be used as a substitute.*

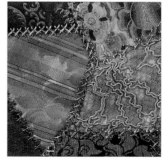

METALLIC-THREAD EMBROIDERY *Metallic hand embroidery threads come as thin strands that can be used together to create just the right thickness for any design. They come in a range of golds, silvers, and bronzes, as well as in colors. Metallic threads with fine cotton threads, in a variety of colors, twisted around them are also available. The metallic threads above are worked in herringbone stitch.*

WOOL-THREAD EMBROIDERY
Wool seam embroidery can only be worked on loosely woven fabrics. This patchwork is made up of wools joined with lapped seams and has no foundation fabric. Fine crewel wools are ideal, since several strands can be used together for just the right thickness.

RIBBON EMBROIDERY *Silk and synthetic embroidery ribbons come in varying widths. Worked through the softer woven fabrics in simple stitches such as those shown above, embroidery ribbon creates a very pretty and appealing effect. These ribbons are now available in a good range of colors.*

BEAD EMBROIDERY *Reserve bead embroidery for small, special crazy-patchwork items that will not require frequent washing. Bead embroidery is worked by threading the beads onto the sewing thread before each stitch is made. The instructions for the stitches shown above are given on page 113.*

COMBINATION STITCHES
Ornate combination stitches worked in stranded cotton floss suit the crazy patches above that were cut from secondhand embroideries. Although they look complicated, combination stitches are made up of very basic stitches worked one at a time in different colors.

MACHINE EMBROIDERY OVER SEAMS

ALTHOUGH machine embroidery is certainly a quick-to-work embellishment for crazy-patch seams, it might require a little practice before you get the hang of it. Your sewing machine manual will give instructions for working elaborate satin stitches or for simple zigzag. Try to use thick threads (and a jeans needle) for bold embellishment.

As with all seam decoration, I advise changing the look of the stitch or the color, or both, on each side of each patch. This will give your patchwork a rich and interesting appearance. Also, use colors that stand out against the fabric.

MACHINE ZIGZAG EMBROIDERY *You don't have to have an expensive machine to work embroidery. This embroidery is a large machine zigzag, worked in a thick, shiny twisted thread. Buttonhole silk works well for this type of seam decoration.*

MACHINE SATIN-STITCH
Special metallic threads for machine embroidery were used on this crazy patchwork. These threads come in a wide range of colors and are plied with other threads for strength and added color. You should consult your sewing machine manual to see what types of satin stitches it can make. See also page 23 for more about machine embroidery.

Ribbon, braids, and beads over seams

All types of braids and ribbons used for trimming dresses, curtains, and upholstery can be used on crazy patchwork. Covering patch seams with these types of trims is probably the easiest and quickest way to finish your patchwork. It also makes the biggest impact on the design because of the width of the braids and ribbons.

Invisible monofilament thread and a machine zigzag stitch are used to secure each side of the ribbons and braids in place. To get extra color variation into your crazy patchworks, you can invent new braids by stitching one on top of another.

Ribbons *Adding tartan ribbons over the seams completely alters this otherwise sedate patchwork. The bows stitched to patch corners give the design a sculptural quality.*

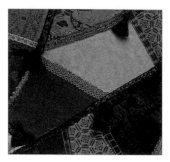

Braids and ribbons *A combination of braids and ribbons were used on this crazy patchwork. Braids add an extra element of texture to the velvet and brocade patch fabrics in the design. Notice how decorating patch seams is an excellent way to use up short lengths of ribbon and braid. (See the opposite page for more information on decorating patch corners.)*

Metallic braids *Metallic braids are used here to cover the joins between the crazy patches on an evening bag (see pages 98–101). Each side of each patch is decorated with a different braid, which enriches this glitzy composition.*

Pinned beads *This technique is worked onto a stuffed heart (see page 23). Beads should be chosen that are compatible with the fabrics: metal or shiny glass beads with silks and rich brocades, and wood, opaque glass, or clay beads with cotton.*

PATCH CORNER DECORATIONS

ANTHING WAS regarded as okay as embellishment on nineteenth-century crazy quilts—buttons, beads, even feathers. Following this tradition, I have used shells, beads, tassels, bows, appliqué, ribbon rosettes, buttons, and charms on my designs. Most of these are ideal for decorating patch corners. Often collisions of seam embroidery, or of ribbons and braids covering seams, create awkward corners on crazy patchwork. Adding decoration helps to hide these untidy areas, but also gives another opportunity to embellish the design with very eye-catching and sometimes unusual details.

Shells are not shown on this page, but there is a good example on the alternative picture on page 45.

BUTTONS, CHARMS, MOTIFS *A metal charm and a sequin motif appear on this patchwork detail. These were used, with metal buttons, to cover the ends of the ribbons and braids on this design (see page 98). Metallic ornaments work well with glitzy fabrics. Whole patchworks could be designed around mother of pearl buttons or around novelty buttons like those on kids' clothes.*

TASSELS *You can purchase tassels to use on your crazy patchwork, or make your own (see page 126). Tassels are best made from pearl cotton, twisted silks, or metallic machine embroidery threads. Very small tassels can also be cut from ready-made tasseled fringe. When adding patch corner decoration, don't feel that you have to attach it to every corner, just spread it out evenly.*

APPLIQUÉ *Machine embroidered motifs ready to iron or stitch over your patch corners can be found in needlecraft shops. You can also make your own motifs by cutting flowers out of floral prints or by cutting out heavily embellished areas of braid, brocades, or lace. Lightweight cutouts can be applied with fusible bonding web (see page 31), but others should be stitched in place.*

RIBBON ROSETTES *Keep odd ends of ribbons to make ribbon rosettes for your crazy patchworks (see page 126).*

QUILT TIES *These small multicolored ties serve a dual purpose: they add a touch of interesting detail and are also a simple traditional technique for holding the quilt layers together. Quilts can also be "tied" with buttons, tassels, or bows.*

EMBROIDERED MOTIFS

Because embroidered motifs are worked onto crazy patches before they are

pieced onto the foundation fabric and because the motifs are small, they provide an excellent

opportunity to experiment with simple embroidery techniques.

THE THING I LOVE ABOUT crazy patchwork is that it is never boring. The little lengths of seam embroidery—a few inches at a time—and the small patch motifs are such a pleasure to work. Even the intricate designs never go on long enough to tire you out.

These small and varied embroideries also provide a great opportunity to experiment. If a technique that is new to you goes wrong on a patch, you don't have to waste much time or fabric; just go on to another patch and try something else. Don't, however, discard fabric scraps with failed experiments on them. Save them to see if you can somehow piece them into your crazy patchwork—minor mistakes can sometimes get lost in all the decoration!

Crazy patchwork is the only patchwork tradition that uses so much embroidery. I always think of them as the embroiderer's patchwork. But this should not discourage the novice embroiderer since the techniques used are very easy to work. And non-embroiderers can use secondhand or ready-made machine-stitched embroideries.

TRANSFERRING LINEAR MOTIFS

LINEAR MOTIFS are elegant and easy to work. Designs can be found in embroidery pattern books, in embroidery magazines, or in stores sold as iron-on transfers. Alternatively, original designs can be used. Think of simple motifs that could personalize your patchwork—your favorite food, flower, car, etc. Even tracing around childrens' hands straight onto the cloth would provide charming linear designs.

Portraits can also be stitched as linear embroidery. All you need is a clear photograph, the larger the better. The face and hair should be traced in simple lines onto tracing paper. If necessary you can then enlarge the design on a photocopier or using the technique on page 35.

Once chosen, the motif is transferred onto the fabric scrap with a water soluble pen using one of the methods given here, then the fabric is mounted in an embroidery hoop and embroidered with a linear stitch such as backstitch or stem stitch (see page 108 for more linear stitches).

METHOD 1 *Trace the motif onto a piece of tracing paper. Then pin the tracing onto a piece of dressmaker's carbon (read the instructions with the carbon carefully to check that it will wash out). Place the motif on the patch fabric and pin it in place. Next, trace the motif using a sharp pencil. Remove the tracing.*

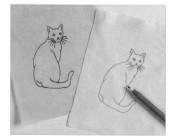

METHOD 2 *If the fabric is light in color, you can transfer the motif directly onto it. Using masking tape, secure the tracing to a window and the patch fabric on top of it. Draw the motif with a water soluble pen. Remove the fabric, mount it in a hoop, and work the stitches in the desired color.*

WORKING CROSS-STITCH OVER WASTE CANVAS

CROSS-STITCH CAN BE worked as a counted-thread stitch onto evenweave fabrics or freehand onto non-evenweaves. Because it is difficult to work freehand cross-stitch evenly, waste canvas can be used as a guide on non-evenweave fabrics allowing you to work cross-stitch easily onto almost any type of fabric. Waste canvas is designed to be quickly pulled away once the stitching is complete.

Any number of cross-stitch designs are available in books and magazines, or you can draw your own onto graph paper using colored pencils. The cross-stitch motifs and letters used for the projects are given on pages 114–116. As with all crazy patchwork embroidery, even the simplest motifs will greatly enliven and enrich your patchwork.

Cross-stitch can create vivid effects on unusual fabrics, such as silk threads on brocades, metallic threads on tafetta, and cotton threads on fine wools. Velvets and other deep pile fabrics should be avoided however, since they tend to encroach onto the stitches and hide them.

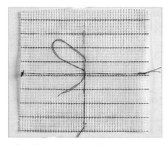

1 *Cut a piece of special waste canvas about 1in (2.5cm) larger all around than the motif. Mark the center of the canvas, by basting a line both vertically and horizontally across it.*

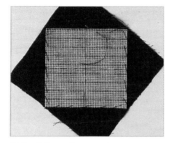

2 *Next, baste the canvas to the patch fabric. Note that canvas does not have to be positioned with its threads parallel to those of the patch; this allows the desired placement on prints and weaves.*

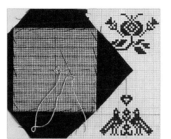

3 *Mount the fabric in an embroidery hoop if desired. Then using a pointed needle, begin at the center and work the design outward over the canvas; avoid piercing the canvas threads.*

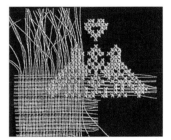

4 *When the motif is complete, remove the basting and trim the canvas around the design close to the embroidery. Dampen the canvas threads, and carefully pull them out, one by one.*

WORKING CROSS-STITCH ON AIDA FABRIC

AIDA IS THE most popular evenweave fabric used for cross-stitch. It is made of cotton and comes in various colors and gauges. It is also available in bands of different widths with plain or colored woven edges. Aida bands can be used for sashing quilts with the woven edges overlapped onto the crazy patchwork.

To enlarge a cross-stitch motif, a larger gauge aida can be used or the stitches can be worked over two or more aida squares. But remember that no matter how many threads a cross-stitch is worked over, it is still represented by only one square on the chart.

RIGHT *Work cross-stitch onto aida in the hand or with the fabric mounted in a hoop. Using a hoop can be easier, as both hands are free to form the stitches, and the fabric cannot be distorted by stitches that are too tight.*

To enlarge the motif on the same gauge fabric, work each cross-stitch over two squares of aida in each direction, but use the thread double or use twice as many strands of floss.

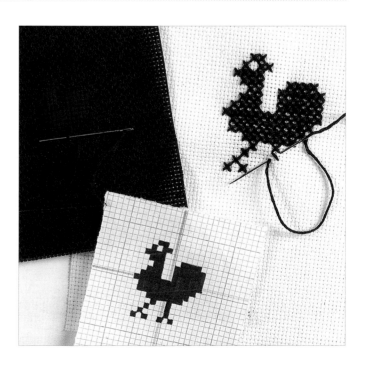

APPLIQUÉ

Appliquéd motifs can be equally effective on your crazy patchwork

as embroidered motifs. Decorating with appliqué is also a quick way to create large,

bold embellishments and add strong flashes of color.

APPLYING GEOMETRIC or pictorial fabric shapes to the ground fabric has long been a decorative technique associated with quilts. It is especially suited to the richly embellished surface of crazy patchwork. As long as the outline is not too intricate, any number of fabric motifs can be used in appliqué—simple geometric shapes, animals, leaves, flowers, butterflies, trees, figures, and even houses are some of the traditional ones.

Most fabrics will work for appliqué as long as they are not too thick and do not unravel easily. If the motif is to be embroidered with details, a solid color might be the best fabric to use; but be sure to experiment with patterned fabrics as well—stripes, checks, plaids, and small-scale prints make striking motifs. Large-scale prints and lace are especially good sources for whole motifs as can be seen in the patchwork shown left and in the instructions that follow.

Appliqué should be stitched to a crazy patch before it is pieced into the patchwork, since the individual patch is easier to handle and maneuver than the whole patchwork.

HANDSTITCHING APPLIQUÉ IN PLACE

THE ORIGINAL WAY to attach an appliqué motif is to turn under the raw edges and stitch the shape in place with invisible slip stitches.

If you are trying out this technique for the first time, use a fabric that is easy to hem and choose a motif with a minimum of curves and points. Transfer your chosen shape onto the appliqué fabric, or, for an instant motif, cut an attractive flower or fruit from a large-scale print. Using fabric prints for appliqué has a long tradition and is called *broderie perse*.

To prevent a dark ground patch from showing through a light-colored motif, press a lightweight fusible interfacing onto the wrong side of the appliqué fabric before using it. Do the same to a fine fabric to give it body, or alternatively stiffen it with spray starch.

When hand stitching appliqué, always attach it to a patch large enough to be mounted on an embroidery hoop or frame. Any extra fabric can be trimmed away when the patch is pieced into your panel of crazy patchwork.

1 *Cut out the motif about* ¹/4in (6mm) *from the outline. Then machine staystitch around the outer edge of the shape. Turn under the seam allowance and baste it in place, clipping and notching any curved edges or inward corners and folding along the staystitching (see above).*

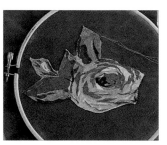

2 *Mount the patch fabric in an embroidery hoop. Slip stitch the appliqué to the patch, using a matching thread. (You may find it helpful to secure the motif with a pin, or with basting, before stitching.) For a decorative edge, embroider the motif in place instead of using slip stitch (see right).*

BONDING APPLIQUÉ IN PLACE

THIS METHOD OF APPLYING appliqué is developed from the traditonal technique of using paste to secure fabric motifs before they are finally edged in place with embroidery stitches or fine braids. Nowadays, paper-backed fusible web is used instead of paste.

The main advantage of bonding is that it is quick. It also eliminates the need to turn under raw edges; this allows the use of more complicated shapes and thicker fabrics, making bonding ideal for intricate motifs cut from fabric prints and lace, and thick embroidered motifs cut from secondhand items. But bonding is just as suitable for drawn shapes, which can be transferred onto the paper side of the web before it is pressed onto the appliqué fabric.

Once an appliqué piece has been bonded to the patch fabric, it is should be secured in place around the edge with hand or machine stitches. Machine satin stitch can be used for a decorative edge, and zigzag stitch in monofilament thread for an invisible attachment.

1 *Cut out a piece of paper-backed fusible web. Then following the manufacturer's instructions, press the glue side of the web onto the wrong side of the appliqué fabric, over the motif.*

2 *Now, leaving the paper backing in place on the wrong side of the appliqué fabric, turn the motif to the right side and carefully cut it out along the design outline, using a sharp pair of scissors.*

3 *Next, remove the paper backing. Press the motif in place on the patch fabric. The appliqué is now ready to be secured with machine stitches. (See below for hand embroidered edging.)*

4 *For a decorative edge, secure the motif with machine satin stitch, using machine embroidery thread (see above). Use machine zigzag and invisible monofilament thread for lace.*

EMBROIDERING THE APPLIQUÉ EDGE

THE RAW EDGES of bonded appliqué need to be covered with machine or hand stitches as explained above.

Although hand embroidery may be more time consuming than machine embroidery, it gives an especially attractive hand-made finish.

Before beginning the hand embroidery, mount the fabric in an embroidery hoop large enough to fit the bonded appliqué motif. Then choose an embroidery thread that will stand out well against both the patch and appliqué fabrics, and use more than one strand if the thread is too fine to show up well.

RIGHT *To hand embroider an appliqué edge, first bond the appliqué in place (see above). Then work blanket stitch, running stitch, or another suitable decorative stitch around the edge over the fold (see right). Before removing the ground fabric from the frame and piecing the patch into your crazy patchwork, work any desired embroidered details onto the appliqué and the ground around it.*

LETTERS AND NUMERALS

Nothing can personalize a crazy patchwork more than inscribing it with signatures,

dates, places, names, and even messages. Here are a selection of techniques for working letters and

numerals on patches before piecing them onto the foundation.

THE IDEA OF SIGNING and dating my crazy patchworks has always appealed to me, as it has to embroiderers through the ages. Think how extra special your needlework becomes when you stitch a dedication onto a patch, such as "To Lucy from Grandma." The crazy patchwork tradition of using needlework for commemoration and dedication will never go out of fashion. Inititals, dates, names, and places can all be used on patchworks that are gifts for weddings, anniversaries, birthdays, births, graduations, in fact for any special event or cherished recipient.

SIGNATURES

IF YOU ARE trying to stitch lettering for the first time, start with your own signature. You won't need any specially designed letters and you will be able to write it as large as required for easy stitching.

Various linear stitches that can be used for working linear script are given on pages 108 and 109. They include running stitch, backstitch, whipped backstitch, split stitch, simple couching, and stem stitch. Experienced embroiderers can also use satin stitch. If your signature becomes too

distorted when you try to write it large, just enlarge your ordinary signature on a photocopier and transfer it to the fabric (see page 28).

RIGHT *Lay a patch fabric large enough to mount in a hoop frame on a firm, flat surface. Then using a water soluble pen, write your signature directly onto the fabric. Be sure to write it large enough to embroider easily. (After mastering the technique you can try to work it smaller later.) Using a thick thread, stitch the signature in split stitch as shown here.*

SATIN-STITCH LETTERS AND NUMERALS

JUST ABOUT ANY TYPE OF lettering or numerals can be worked in satin stitch, and all styles of letters are to be found in ordinary books, magazines, and even newspapers. For more traditional alphabets, old needlecraft books are good sources. There is one such traditional alphabet on page 117, which is especially useful for monograms.

Satin stitch lettering requires a little practice to perfect. Although flat satin stitch letters can look attractive, the best effect is achieved by tramming or padding the stitch as

shown in the steps below. This is the traditional method used for monograms. It produces fine, distinct, and sculptural initials, and the raised stitches catch the light beautifully. I use silk threads as often as possible for satin-stitched letters; they give a luster and sense of luxury to all the beautiful old fabrics incorporated into my crazy patchworks.

Untrammed satin stitch is a good technique to use for copying enlarged handwriting, since it can imitate the thin and thick variations in the lines.

1 *Trace the chosen letter (or numeral) and transfer it onto the patch fabric using one of the methods given on page 28. Make sure that the patch fabric is big enough to be stretched onto a hoop.*

2 *Mount the fabric in the hoop frame. Using a thick twisted thread, work the outlines in small backstitches. (These stitches are essential for giving the final letter smooth, even edges.)*

3 *Using several strands of floss, cover the fabric inside the outlines with straight stitches, working in the direction opposite to the one the final satin stitches will be worked.*

4 *Using a thick twisted thread such as pearl cotton or silk, cover the letter with satin stitches. The initial under-tramming saves time and stitching in the final luxurious thread.*

CROSS-STITCH LETTERS

ARDENT CROSS-STITCH embroiderers will probably have collected cross-stitch magazines and books full of cross-stitch alphabets to work from. The traditional signing alphabet is given on page 114; it is included for the words on the baby quilt on pages 60–63.

The number of strands of thread needed for working cross-stitch depends on the size of the stitch and the thickness of the thread. Thick twisted threads such as pearl cotton might be thick enough to use singly, whereas several strands of cotton or silk floss will be required. It is best to test

working with your chosen thread until you get a nice plump cross-stitch. Some traditional folk cross-stitch was worked so thick that it is hard to tell at first glance that it is cross-stitch, but these glossy fat stitches are incredibly appealing.

It might seem quite time-consuming to work messages on crazy patches, but they can be worked quite large by increasing the size of the individual stitches. Bits of embroidered words or letters or words cut from old samplers that you have worked in the past or from secondhand pieces can also be used.

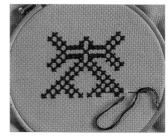

ON EVENWEAVE AIDA *This very ornate letter "A" is shown here being worked on a colored aida fabric. To work on aida, first mount the patch fabric in a hoop. If the aida is a fine gauge, or for a large letter, work each cross-stitch over two aida squares in each direction, using several strands of floss. See page 109 for how to work cross-stitch.*

OVER WASTE CANVAS *To work a cross-stitch letter onto a non-evenweave fabric, use waste canvas. Instructions for using waste canvas are given on page 29. Note that the top arm of cross-stitch can be worked in either direction, slanting to the right or to the left, as long as all the stitches in each motif are worked in the same direction.*

MULTIPLE-LINE LETTERS

ANYONE CAN work this type of multiple-line lettering onto a crazy patch, and it doesn't require a pre-designed alphabet. The initial letter is drawn in simple lines, each with a slight curve (see right), but any style could be used. Drawing letters directly onto the fabric will give the lines character, but you can, if you prefer, draw them on paper and transfer them using one of the methods given on page 28.

This technique is a good way to create large letters quickly; there is no limit to the size of the letter. Larger letters can be worked by increasing the number of lines on each side of the

initial letter. The multiple lines can be worked spaced apart, as here, or worked close together so no background shows through. Any linear stitch can be used to embroider the lines.

A good variation on this design would be an outline in a line stitch and the inside filled with another type of stitch pattern.

It sounds obvious, but always remember that the larger the stitch on crazy patch embroideries, the fatter the thread should be. The stitches must look strong against the background patches. Pearl cotton or a thick twisted silk work well, or several strands of embroidery floss.

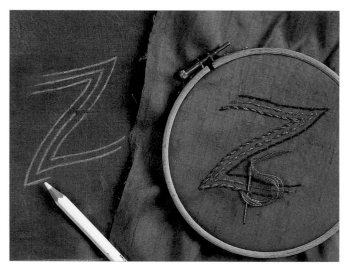

ABOVE *Draw a large letter directly onto the fabric, using a water soluble pen for light colored fabrics, or dressmaker's chalk pencil for dark ones. Then draw a parallel line on each side of the first line and about ⅛in (3mm) away. Mount the fabric in a hoop and work the central line in running stitch using a light shade. Work the other two lines in backstitch using a dark shade. Then whip one of the dark backstitch lines with the light shade to create a medium shade.*

BLOCK LETTERS AND NUMERALS

LARGE, SMOOTH, bold sans serif block headline letters or logos can be worked on crazy patches in trammed satin stitch. This technique is similar to the technique shown on page 33, which is used for delicate monograms, but is specifically designed with thick letters and numerals in mind. The direction of the final satin stitches is the most important part of the technique. It is the direction of the stitches and the use of a shiny twisted thread that makes the padded shapes reflect the light so effectively. Pearl cotton or silk embroidery threads work best.

Silk and cotton floss are also very shiny but would catch and snag easily and do not create the type of attractive ridged texture that twisted threads do.

When choosing thread colors for your embroidered letters and numerals, try to pick a color that will stand out boldly against the patch fabric color. If in doubt, try out one letter or numeral, then pin it on the wall, stand back, and study the contrast. Then reverse the color of the thread and fabric and study this. Your experiments can be included as small patches in your final crazy patchwork.

1 *Design your own numbers (or letters) or trace them from a book, newspaper, or magazine. If necessary, enlarge found letters as explained below. Ensure that the thickness of the number or letter does not exceed $^3/_4$–1in (2–2.5cm) in width. Position numbers for dates equidistant from each other, and plan the direction of the final satin stitches on paper.*

2 *Transfer the numbers to the patch fabric, and mount in a hoop. Work the outlines in backstitch using a thick twisted thread such as pearl cotton, then fill in with straight stitches using several strands of floss and working the stitches in the opposite direction to those of the final stitches. Work satin stitches over the tramming stitches, using the twisted thread.*

APPLIQUÉ LETTERS

VERY LARGE letters or numbers can be made for crazy patches using the appliqué technique. Depending on your appliqué skills, any large letter shapes can be made into appliqué cutouts.

When choosing fabric for an appliqué letter, consider the texture as well as the color. A texture that contrasts with that of the patch fabric will make the letter stand out better and add interest to the detail.

Once bonded to the patch, the letter should be edged with hand or machine embroidery. A hand buttonhole or satin stitch edging works well but is very time consuming. Machine zigzag is the smartest finish and is

quicker to work. For an even outline, place the machine needle at the edge of the appliqué and work the zigzag stitch inward.

RIGHT *Find a block letter in a newspaper or magazine, cut it out, and glue it to a piece of paper. To enlarge the letter, first draw a regular grid over the letter. Then draw a larger grid and slowly pencil in the letter on it, matching the shape of the line in each square. Use this enlargement to make an appliqué cutout. Bond the cutout to the patch fabric following the instructions on page 31. Cover the edge of the letter with a close machine zigzag in a thick thread.*

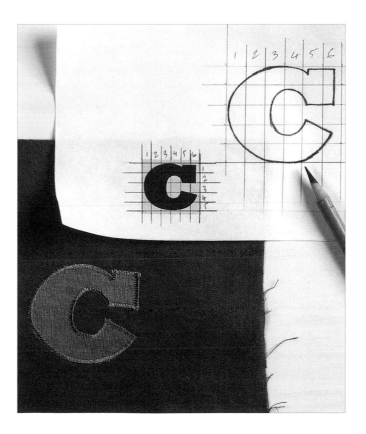

COUNTRY COLLECTION

The Country Collection illustrates how very simple fabric and color combination can make highly successful crazy patchwork with a contemporary flavor.

THIS COLLECTION uses simple, crisp color combinations—a departure from the fabrics and colors often associated with crazy patchwork, although many traditional quilts were made from basic cotton fabrics cut from old workclothes and household linens. Pared-down trims—check and plaid ribbons, rickrack, flat buttons, wooden beads, and shells—add just the right finishing touches for this clean, fresh country look that fits comfortably into present-day interiors. Most of the projects in this chapter would make ideal introductions to crazy patchwork for novices. All of them are fairly easy to work, and the fabrics used are widely available. The Button Picture uses simple running stitch as the decorative seam edging, and the Cross-stitch Cushion is embellished with small, uncomplicated embroidery. Designed more in the spirit of Crazy Patchwork, the wool throw and stuffed heart are surprisingly simple to make. These designs, along with alternatives that appear with the instructions, open up a range of new possibilities for contemporary crazy patchworks.

CROSS-STITCH CUSHION

Marrying the lively geometry and the fine embroidery of traditional crazy patchwork with clean, crisp modern red-and-white fabric prints and weaves, this design surely shows off contemporary crazy patchwork at its best.

THE CROSS-STITCH motifs on this crazy-patch cushion are worked over waste canvas onto the patches before they are basted onto a cotton foundation fabric, secured with invisible machine stitching, and edged with simple herringbone-stitch embroidery.

The types of patterned and plain fabric scraps used should not be difficult to find and you might even have some in your remnant collection. It is a good idea though to take the time to find a few unusual ribbons to add that extra special touch to the arrangement.

LEFT *The strong jewel reds, whites, and off-whites of this crazy patchwork create an intense contrast, a contrast only slightly tempered by the subtle introduction of two plaid patches with beige tones. The delicate cross-stitch motifs stand out beautifully against the sharp geometry of the patch shapes and the straight lines of the fabric patterns.*

RIGHT *The finished Cross-stitch Cushion measures 18in (46cm) square. If desired, enlarge or reduce the size of your cushion by changing the size of the foundation fabric the patches are stitched to.*

MATERIALS FOR THE CUSHION

ABOVE *The pearl cotton embroidery threads in ruby red, off-white, and variegated red, and a selection of the red-and-white cottons, linens, and wide ribbons in solids, checks, plaids, stripes, and dots used on the Cross-stitch Cushion.*

You will need

- **Crazy-patch scraps** ~ red and white cottons, linens, and wide ribbons in solids, checks, plaids, stripes, and dots (see sample fabrics at left and photographs of cushion for ideas)
- **Foundation fabric** ~ strong cotton fabric in white
- **Embroidery thread** ~ pearl cotton embroidery thread in off-white, ruby red, and a variegated red that ranges from pink to dark red
- **Waste canvas** ~ 11-stitches-to-the-inch (2.5cm) waste canvas, for cross-stitch embroidery on fabric patches
- **Sewing threads** ~ basting thread, invisible monofilament thread, and matching thread for backing
- **Cushion cover back** ~ piece of one of red-and-white patch fabrics
- **Pillow form** ~ to fit cushion cover
- **Fasteners** ~ snaps or zipper for cushion cover opening (optional)

MAKING THE CUSHION PATCHWORK

CHOOSE YOUR PATCH scraps carefully before contemplating starting your project. Reds are sometimes too sharp and metallic in appearance, so hold out for warm, jewel reds in various intensities. If in doubt about your choices, lay roughly cut patches on the table or pin them on a wall, then step back and study the effect. Discard any scraps you are unsure of, and add others until the mixture looks just right. The cross-stitch will stand out best if worked on a solid-colored ground, so be sure to introduce a few plain red, white, or off-white patches. For an alternative color scheme in blues and whites based on blue jeans, see the alternative patchwork on the opposite page.

1 Before beginning the patchwork, work cross-stitch motifs on several solid-colored patches. Use your own cross-stitch designs or the ones shown here, which are given on page 116. Baste a piece of waste canvas onto the center of a patch. Then, beginning at the center of the motif work the cross-stitch design over the canvas using pearl cotton embroidery thread in a contrasting color. Remove the waste canvas as explained on page 29.

Beginners should work the cross-stitch on an embroidery hoop. When using a hoop, make sure that the patch is big enough to fit the hoop; the excess fabric can be trimmed away before the patch is sewn to the foundation fabric.

2 To prepare the cotton foundation fabric, draw an 18in (46cm) square onto it using a water soluble pen and a ruler. Then draw a second line 3/4in (2cm) outside the first to indicate the position of the seam allowance. Decide on the positions for the embroidered patches inside the outlines, then begin arranging the patches at one corner. Trim the patch edges so that they fit together and overlap each other about 1/4in (6mm). Pin the patches in place as they are positioned, then baste along the raw edges, removing the pins as you stitch.

3 After basting the patches to the cotton foundation fabric, secure them with machine stitches. Thread the sewing machine with invisible monofilament thread, including the bobbin (see page 22 for more about monofilament thread). Set the machine to a medium-sized zigzag stitch, and if desired, test the stitch size on a piece of scrap fabric before working on the patchwork. Then work machine zigzag stitches over the raw edges between the patches (see page 22 for detailed instructions for this method of piecing crazy patches).

4 Continue in this way, basting and machine stitching the patches in place on the cotton foundation fabric, and introducing ribbon patches at random, until the foundation has been completely covered, including the seam allowance. Remove the basting along the raw edges of the patches. Then thread an embroidery needle with ruby red or variegated red pearl cotton embroidery thread, and work herringbone stitch over the joins between the patches. (Instructions for herringbone stitch are given on page 111.)

CROSS-STITCH CUSHION • *Country Collection*

5 If desired, work the embroidery with the patchwork mounted on an embroidery hoop. Although the foundation fabric and the zigzag stitching gives the patchwork a certain firmness, some might still find it easier to stitch the embroidery with the fabric stretched on a frame. This leaves both hands free to stitch and provides an extra-firm surface to work on. If using a hoop, move it as necessary after each area has been completed.

Continue covering the joins between the patches with herringbone stitch, varying the thread color at random. When all the embroidery has been completed, lay the patchwork face down on a padded surface and press lightly on the wrong side. Then trim the edges of the patchwork to straighten them if necessary, ensuring that the corners are square. Turn to page 122 for instructions on how to stitch on the backing and complete the cushion cover.

PATCHWORK ALTERNATIVES

SUBTLE CHANGES could be made to the Cross-stitch Cushion to make it easier and quicker to stitch, but just as striking in design. For instance, the cross-stitch motifs could be replaced by simple flower appliqués in pinks and reds, cut from bold floral prints. Or, the machine zigzagging and hand embroidery along the patch edges could be omitted, and instead the scraps could be machine topstitched (see right), allowing the raw edges to fray and adding extra texture to the crazy patches.

RIGHT *This alternative color scheme is much softer than that of the bold red-and-white Cross-stitch Cushion. Striped, checked, and plain patches in faded denims, muted navys, and whites are machine-edged with yellow topstitching which picks out the yellow cross-stitching.*

BUTTON PICTURE

Only a few small scraps of various neutral shades of linens are needed

to make this clever button picture. The crazy patches are joined to the foundation fabric with simple

running stitch using linen embroidery threads.

THIS BUTTON PICTURE is a good project for a crazy patchwork beginner. Because it is small, it can be made quite quickly and without a sewing machine. In addition, it requires a minimal amount of fabric scraps, which can be taken from old napkins or other table linen that would otherwise have been thrown out due to staining. The beauty of linen scraps is that they sometimes have interesting selvages that can be incorporated into the crazy

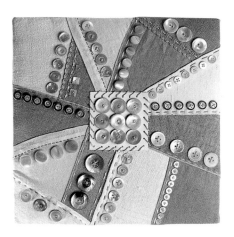

patchwork as design features. Existing decorative openwork hem stitching on scraps cut from secondhand linens can be used in the same way.

LEFT *After being decorated, the patchwork is glued to a padded mount. The finished linen Button Picture measures 12in by 12in (30cm by 30cm).*
RIGHT *The soft, dullish sheen of the linens contrasts beautifully with the shimmering mother-of-pearl on this crazy patchwork.*

MATERIALS FOR THE PICTURE

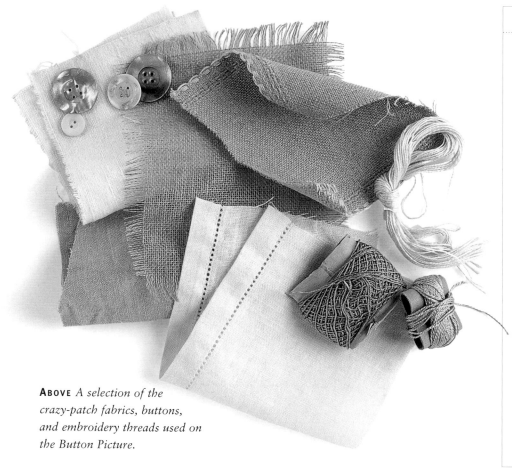

ABOVE *A selection of the crazy-patch fabrics, buttons, and embroidery threads used on the Button Picture.*

You will need

- **Crazy-patch scraps** ~ fine and coarse linen fabrics in an assortment of neutral shades
- **Foundation fabric** ~ white or neutral-colored strong cotton fabric
- **Embroidery thread** ~ linen threads (or pearl cotton) in three or four neutral shades, for joining patches
- **Buttons** ~ an assortment of small mother-of-pearl buttons in groups of about six for decorating patch seams; plus a set of about nine buttons stitched to a $3\frac{1}{8}$in (8cm) square of cardboard, for center of picture
- **Special tool** ~ small hole punch
- **Picture mount** ~ piece of strong cardboard 12in (30cm) square
- **Padding** ~ piece of thick felt or piece of polyester batting same size as cardboard picture mount
- **Backing** ~ piece of beige linen 14in (35cm) square
- **Fabric glue** ~ for attaching completed patchwork to cardboard mount

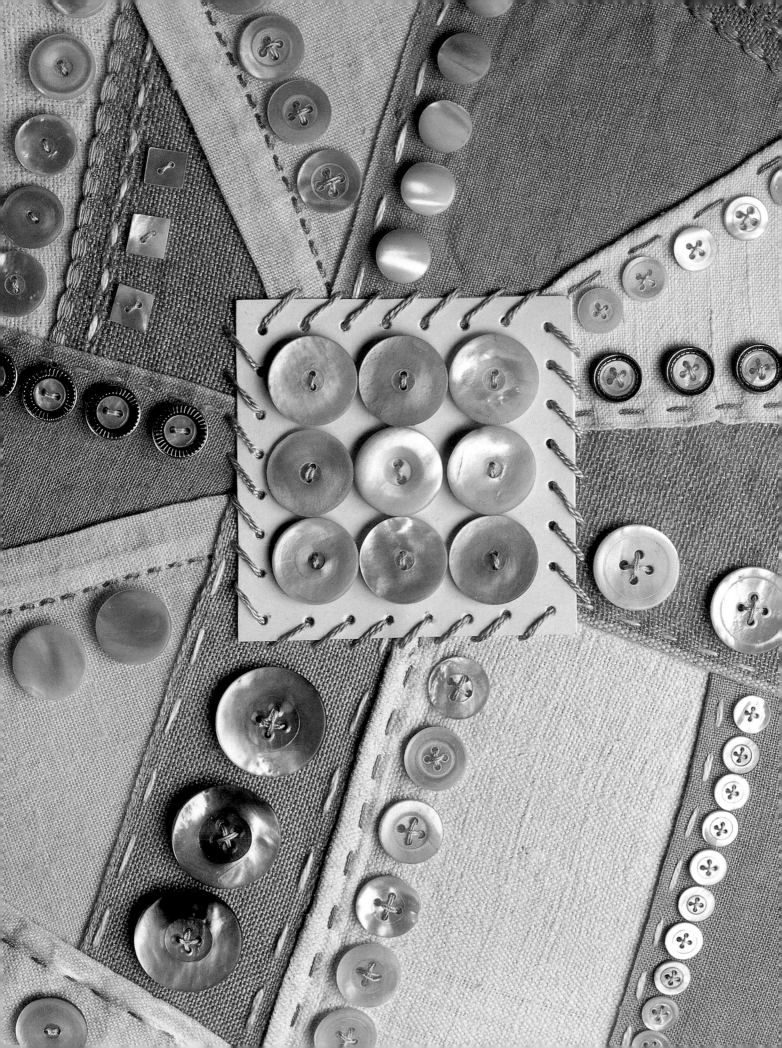

Making the picture patchwork

Take your time when deciding on the arrangement for the linen crazy patches. Try to integrate the interesting hems and selvages of your scraps into the design by lapping them over the raw edges of other patches. Since changing the fabric and button positions can greatly alter the overall look of the picture, keep trying different layouts until the arrangement looks balanced—with the dark and light tones evenly distributed. The extra time spent is well worth it.

When working the large decorative running stitches along the edges of the patches, use two strands of embroidery thread to make the stitching stand out if necessary. (See page 108 for how to work running stitch.)

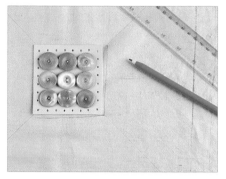

1 Using the 12in (30cm) square piece of cardboard, trace the finished picture size onto the foundation fabric. Add a second outline 1in (2.5cm) from first for the hem allowance. Then draw diagonal lines from corner to corner of the square. Use the small card of buttons to trace the center of the picture.

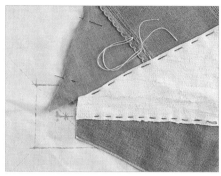

2 Piece the patches in place around the center square, overlapping the center square and covering the hem allowance. Using a contrasting tone of embroidery thread and running stitch, secure the patches in place along the selvages or folded edges of the scraps (see page 23 for this hand piecing technique).

3 When all the patches have been hand stitched to the foundation fabric, press the crazy patchwork on the wrong side. Then arrange the sets of buttons along the seam lines, making sure that they do not cover the decorative running stitches. Stitch the buttons in place using the embroidery thread.

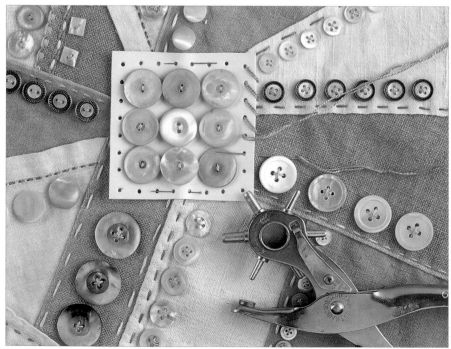

4 Using a pencil, lightly mark the positions for punch holes around the card of buttons $3/8$in (1cm) apart and $1/4$in (5mm) from the edge. Then carefully punch the holes over the marked positions. Place the card in the center of the crazy patchwork and using a doubled strand of the embroidery thread, stitch it in place as shown above.

5 To fit the 12in (30cm) cardboard mount, the completed piece of crazy patchwork should measure at least 14in by 14in (35cm by 35cm) including the hem allowance which will be glued to the back of the mount. Trim the raw outer edges of the patchwork to straighten if necessary. The piece is now ready to stretch onto a padded cardboard mount. Turn to page 122 for the padding, mounting, and backing instructions.

PATCHWORK ALTERNATIVES

A GOOD ALTERNATIVE for the mother-of-pearl Button Picture design would be a picture made up of colored buttons and solid fabric patches in complementary shades. Or the theme of the picture could be changed from buttons to shells.

BELOW *While retaining the neutral-colored linen patches of the original Button Picture, this alternative crazy patchwork uses an attractive range of shells instead of buttons as the seam decoration. The shells add rosy pinks and bright corals to*

the otherwise sedate fabric color scheme. To make this alternative picture, select sets of shells that are pierced so that they can be stitched in place covering the seams, and choose a large, iridescent mother-of-pearl shell for the centerpiece.

EMBROIDERED LAUNDRY BAG

This large bag is made from generously-sized patches, so it can be pieced very quickly

on the sewing machine. The handsome original backstitch motifs are hand embroidered onto the

scraps before they are joined together on the foundation.

A S WITH ALL CRAZY patchwork, the more effort put into choosing the right patch fabrics, the better and more satisfying the end result will be. The blues carefully chosen for this bag all have a soft, slightly faded appearance. The whites fabrics selected are also toned down ones, and the only really crisp, sharp white is the purposely bright rickrack trim. Make sure that the major colors of fabrics are blue and white. Too many bright additional colors will detract from the simple line embroidery.

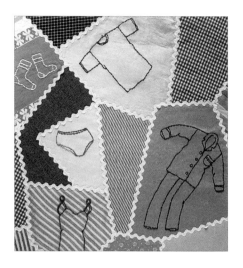

LEFT *Bicolor blue-and-white crazy patchwork works well when enough blue tones are included to keep the composition lively. To see the other motifs and fabrics used on this design, and for an alternative color scheme for a bag, see page 49.*

RIGHT *The finished Embroidered Laundry Bag measures 18in (46cm) wide by 27in (69cm) tall. A strong white drawstring cord is threaded through a machine-stitched casing at the top of the bag. Forming both the top border of the bag and the inside of the bag, the lining is cut from a navy-and-white cotton gingham.*

MATERIALS FOR THE BAG

ABOVE *A selection of the crazy-patch fabric scraps, the white rickrack, and the three shades of pearl cotton embroidery thread used on the Embroidered Laundry Bag.*

You will need

- **Crazy-patch scraps** ~ blue and white cottons in a range of fabric types, including chambrey, prints, ginghams, solids, and textured weaves (see left)
- **Foundation fabric** ~ strong cotton fabric in white
- **Embroidery thread** ~ pearl cotton embroidery thread in white, dark blue, and variegated blue, for embroidered backstitch motifs
- **Seam decoration** ~ approximately 4yd (4$\frac{1}{2}$m) of white rickrack for decorating patch seams
- **Sewing threads** ~ basting thread, invisible monofilament thread, and matching thread for sewing lining
- **Lining** ~ piece of navy and white check cotton fabric 37in (95cm) by 37in (95cm)
- **Cords** ~ 2$\frac{1}{4}$yd (2m) of white cotton cord for drawstring and bag strap (ends of cord can be unraveled for tassels)

Making the bag patchwork

The Embroidered Laundry Bag is made from a single rectangular piece of crazy patchwork. Because the completed patchwork is folded widthwise when it is made up into a bag, take extra time to plan the positioning of the embroidered patches so that they are evenly distributed. Use the finished patchwork shown in Step 5 and the finished bag pictured on page 47 as guides to the embroidery positions.

Do not try to match your patch shapes to those shown in the steps, since it would not be worth the extra time. One of the charms of crazy patchwork is the random shapes.

1 Before beginning the patchwork, choose a few motifs to work onto patch scraps. Use your own motifs or the ones given on page 118. Following the instructions on page 28, transfer each motif onto a patch large enough to mount on an embroidery hoop.

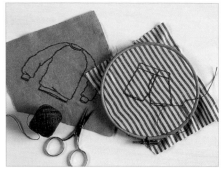

2 Next, mount the piece of fabric onto the embroidery hoop. Using one strand of pearl cotton embroidery thread that contrasts with the ground fabric, work the outlines of the motif in a bold backstitch. Embroider nine or ten more crazy patches in this way.

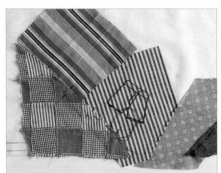

3 Using a water soluble pen, mark the size of the finished bag patchwork on the foundation fabric, by drawing a rectangle 36in (92cm) by 18in (46cm). Then add a second line outside the first and ³⁄₄in (2cm) from it, for the seam allowance. Next, decide on the positions for the embroidered scraps on the foundation fabric. Note that the bottom of the bag is along a long edge and that the patchwork piece will be folded widthwise, so the embroidery should be positioned accordingly. Pin and baste the first few patches in place, overlapping the raw patch edges by at least ¹⁄₄in (6mm) and ensuring that the foundation fabric seam allowance is being completely covered by the fabric scraps. Machine zigzag stitch the joins between the patches with invisible monofilament thread. (See page 22 for more about this piecing technique.)

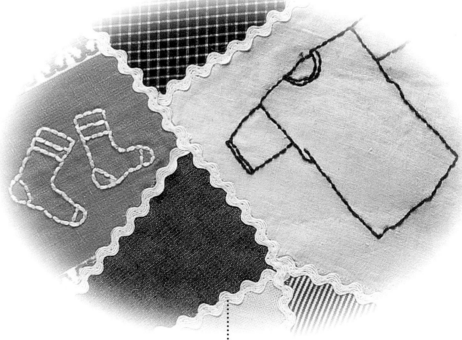

4 When the patches have all been zigzagged to the foundation fabric, remove the basting. Baste strips of rickrack over the joins between the patches. Where possible tuck the raw ends of the rickrack under an adjacent rickrack, turning under the raw ends only where it is unavoidable. Using monofilament thread, machine zigzag down the center of the rickrack to secure it.

5 When all the rickrack has been machine stitched in place, remove the basting. Then trim the finished patchwork to measure 37in (95cm) by 19in (49cm), ensuring that the corners are cut square. This allows for a $^1/_2$in (1.5cm) seam allowance around the edge of the patchwork. Next, place the patchwork face down on a padded surface, and press lightly on the wrong side with a steam iron. Embroidery should always be pressed on a padded surface so that is will not be flattened. Turn to page 123 for how to finish the bag.

PATCHWORK ALTERNATIVES

IF YOU WANT TO personalize your crazy patchwork project, try altering the design provided to suit your tastes. For instance, why not choose an alternative color scheme for your laundry bag. Or, you could work different types of backstitch motifs onto the patches, such as simple animal shapes or large flowers and leaves. Select a theme that suits the person the bag is intended for. For alternative embroidery stitches, try any of the linear stitches given in the Stitch Library on pages 108 and 109. Running stitch motifs would be especially quick to work, but when using running stitch be sure to use a thick embroidery thread so that the outlines stand out. For an alternative trim, consider narrow striped or plaid ribbons to replace the rickrack over the patch seams.

RIGHT *This alternative patchwork was designed for a large toy bag. To make it, follow the instructions given for the Embroidered Laundry Bag, but look for colorful ginghams and plaids like those shown here. The templates for the motifs are given on page 119, along with an explanation of what types of stitches to use. Work the embroidery with stranded embroidery floss in several colors.*

GINGHAM HEART

This precious crazy-patchwork heart was made from a little girl's baby clothes as an

extra-special keepsake. The stuffed heart is prepared first and the patches are pinned rather than

stitched in place. The pins are adorned with brightly colored beads.

THIS HEART HONORS the crazy-patchwork tradition of using fabric scraps that have resonant personal memories. What better way to make use of old, but treasured, baby's or children's clothes, evening wear that reminds one of a special event, or even bridal clothes, than to piece them into a keepsake heart. If you are reluctant to cut into those special fabrics for such a small item, why not cut small scraps from deep dress hems, thereby leaving the garments intact. Or, make a larger item from the clothes, such as a

pair of matching crazy-patch cushion covers, a small quilt throw, or a baby quilt (see the quilt on page 60 and the quilt instructions on page 124.)

LEFT *It is hard to believe that the patches on this heart were cut from worn and washed baby clothes. The fabric colors still look crisp, and the brightly colored beads give them even more intensity.*
RIGHT *The heart measures 8in (20cm) from top to tip and about 8$\frac{1}{2}$in (22cm) across the widest part. The ribbon at the top is for hanging the heart to display it.*

MATERIALS FOR THE HEART

ABOVE *The plaid edging ribbon, a selection of the linen and cotton check, plaid, and small-scale print fabrics, and some of the wooden and glass beads used on the keepsake Gingham Heart. (See the Beaded Heart on page 72 for tips on purchasing large and small beads for pinning.)*

You will need

- **Crazy-patch scraps** ~ linen and cotton plaids, checks, and small-scale prints, all in a range of bright colors
- **Heart fabric** ~ piece of felt 12in (30cm) by 24in (61cm) for making stuffed heart
- **Stuffing** ~ sawdust (from pet store) for stuffing felt heart
- **Backing** ~ piece of small-scale bicolor plaid for covering back of heart
- **Sewing threads** ~ matching threads for sewing felt heart and attaching backing fabric
- **Appliqué** ~ shapes are cut from patch fabrics
- **Fusible web** ~ paper-backed fusible web, for bonding appliqué
- **Pins** ~ tarnish-proof lace pins
- **Beads** ~brightly colored large, medium, and small glass and wooden beads
- **Ribbon** ~ narrow plaid ribbon for edging heart, and a wide plaid ribbon for hanging heart (optional)

MAKING THE HEART PATCHWORK

THE INSTRUCTIONS for making the stuffed heart base for this patchwork are given at the back of the book. Ensure when making the heart that you stuff it as tightly as recommended.

Before the fabric scraps are pinned to the front of the heart, the decorative backing fabric is stitched in place. Then each of the crazy patches is decorated with appliqué (see pages 30 and 31 for more about appliqué techniques).

You will see that the floral cutouts for the heart were cut from a piece of machine-embroidered plaid. If you want to imitate the effect, trace the motif given on page 119 onto the front of a scrap and work the petal lines in backstitch. Then bond fusible web to the wrong side of the motif, and with the right side facing, cut out the flower close to the backstitch.

1 First, make the felt stuffed heart (see page 123) and use the template on page 119 to cut out the plaid backing on the bias. Clipping the seam allowance as necessary, stretch and pin the backing to one side of the heart close to the felt seam. Then trim the seam allowance slightly. Overcast the raw edges of the backing fabric to the felt seam allowances. This seam will eventually be covered by the ribbon edging.

2 For the appliqué cutouts, trace a star, a heart, or a flower onto the paper side of a piece of fusible web, using the templates given on page 119. Bond the web onto the wrong side of a fabric scrap, carefully following the manufacturer's instructions. With the wrong side facing, cut out the shape. Prepare as many motifs as required. (To imitate the machine-embroidered plaid shown here, see the introduction at the left.)

3 After all the appliqués have been prepared, remove the paper backing from each of the star, heart, and flower motifs. (You will need about ten or eleven motifs for this size heart, unless you are using motifs smaller than those used here.) Next, select contrasting patch-fabric groundings for each of the cutouts. If in doubt, lay the patches side-by-side and arrange the cutouts on top of them. Rearrange a few times to study how the effect changes with each arrangement. (Tilt the motifs so that the lines of the plaids and checks on the cutouts do not line up with those of the ground fabric.) When you have decided on which ground to use for each cutout, fuse the appliqué to the patches.

4 Begin arranging the patches on the heart. As the patches are positioned, trim them to fit and fold under each overlapping edge, turning 1/4in (6mm) to the wrong side (see page 23 for more about piecing crazy patches). Use pins to hold the patches in place.

5 When the patches are in position, begin pinning on the beads. At each patch corner pin a large contrasting bead with a small bead on top of it. (Use the same bead colors for each patch corner to unify the design.) Pin medium-sized beads along the folds, leaving gaps between the beads and changing the colors of the beads on each side of each patch. Along the edges of the appliqué motifs, pin small beads, using a color that tones in with the appliqué motifs (for instance, red beads for a red motif). Leave smaller gaps between these small beads. Then pin a large bead with a small bead on top of it to the center of each appliqué motif, using contrasting beads so that they stand out.

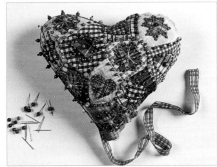

To display the finished Gingham Heart, you might like to hang it on the wall. You will need at least a yard (meter) of a wide plaid ribbon. Place the center of the ribbon at the center of the top of the heart and stitch in place (see below). Tie a bow about 5in (13cm) from the heart and trim the ends.

6 Continue arranging crazy patches and beading them in place in this way until patches cover the entire front of the stuffed heart and overlap the felt heart seam. Next, pin the raw patch edges around the edge of the heart at the heart seam line as shown above. When pinning, ease in the excess fabric around the outward curves. Push the pins into the heart, then carefully trim the edges close to the seam line.

7 To finish the heart, cover the raw edges where the patches meet the backing with a patterned ribbon. Place the end of the ribbon over the center of the top of the heart and begin wrapping it around the heart, pinning it in place. Then using large beads with small beads on top of them, bead the ribbon in place. When the center top of the heart is reached, cut off the excess ribbon, fold under the end, and pin it in place.

PATCHWORK ALTERNATIVES

IF YOUR COLLECTION of fabric remnants does not yield the colors and types of plaids and checks used on the Gingham Heart, try making up your own crazy patch arrangement in a different color scheme and using small-scale prints, stripes, or solids, or a combination of all three. Choose your bead colors carefully, making sure that some complement or match your patches and some contrast with them. For more elaborate and luxurious stuffed heart crazy patchwork, see the silk designs on pages 73 and 75.

RIGHT *Solid, patterned, striped, and checked blue and white cotton crazy patches cover this alternative heart. Off-white, dark blue, and sand-colored glass and wooden beads complete the restrained color palette. Note the interestingly different ways the star motifs have been beaded. To make a heart in this color scheme, follow the instructions for the stuffed Gingham Heart, or cover a polystyrene foam heart.*

EMBROIDERED WOOL THROW

This crazy-patch project couldn't be simpler, since there are no real patches involved. The mock patchwork is merely embroidered onto a solid-colored wool fabric. The traditional use of lively combination stitches creates an energetic and bold composition.

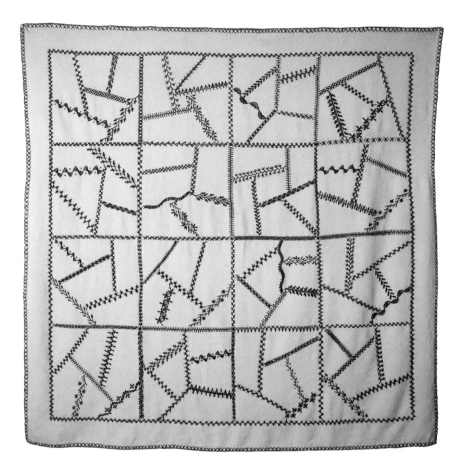

Mock crazy patches can be just as exciting to make as the real thing, and in half the time! Hopefully this design will inspire you to try other types of mock crazy-patch arrangements that are equally as quick to work. For instance, you could use a mohair-mix fabric for the throw and create the random "patches" with colorful plain or patterned ribbons machine zigzagged in place with invisible thread. And a wide ribbon could be folded over the edge to bind it.

Left *The finished Embroidered Wool Throw measures 67in (165cm) square. See page 56 for altering the size.*
Right *The throw is embroidered almost entirely with bold combination stitches worked in two colors. A few wide stitches—sheaf, cretan, feathered chain, and wheatear—are also used individually but the thread color along these stitches is changed frequently for variety.*

MATERIALS FOR THE THROW

Right *A piece of the cream wool material and the red and blue tapestry wool yarn used on the Embroidered Wool Throw. Be sure to choose a loosely woven wool fabric, because the thick tapestry embroidery yarn will not pass very easily through the more closely woven wools.*

You will need

- **Blanket** ~ plain cream wool blanket trimmed to measure 66in (168cm) square, or cream wool fabric same size
- **Embroidery thread** ~ tapestry wool embroidery yarn in red and blue
- **Special materials** ~ graph paper or sewing pattern-paper, water soluble pen, and ruler for planning
- **Sewing thread** ~ contrasting basting thread for mapping out "patch" divisions and "seam lines" on blanket
- **Special needle** ~ tapestry needle

MAKING THE MOCK PATCHWORK

THE PIECE OF WOOL blanket used to make this throw was trimmed to measure 66in (168cm) square. To change the size of the throw, just plan your block arrangement carefully, following the instructions in the first step.

As a rule, the smallest size for a generous throw is about 48in (122cm) wide by 66in (168cm) long, before the edge is turned under. A square shape is, however, easier to plan. If you want to embroider a full-sized blanket, either purchase one that is the desired size or use your bed as a guide to the required measurements. Always plan the blanket layout before cutting your wool.

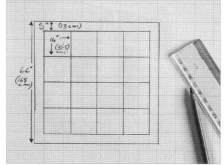

1 Before beginning the lines of stitching on the blanket, plan the positioning of the embroidery on a sheet of graph paper, or a large piece of squared pattern paper. First, draw the outline of the throw *to scale* on the paper. Then, for a square blanket, draw a line about 4in (10cm) to 5in (13cm) inside the outline for the position of the border. Next, bisect the square horizontally and vertically. Lastly, divide each quarter into four squares and mark the measurements on the drawing. If your throw is rectangular, plan and draw the center squares before drawing the border outline, and trim off any excess around the edge of the throw if necessary.

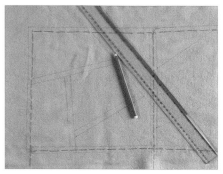

2 Carefully following the plan on the graph paper and using a contrasting basting thread, first baste the border line around the edge of the blanket about 5in (13cm) from the raw edge, then baste the lines that divide the blanket into squares. Next, using a water soluble pen and a ruler, draw the lines of the mock random "crazy patches" inside the first square on the blanket, making each "patch" a generous size in order to accommodate the wide lines of embroidery. To mark the guide lines for the embroidery stitches—about ¹/₂in (1.5cm) wide—draw parallel lines, using a water soluble pen. Draw a different patch arrangement in the next block.

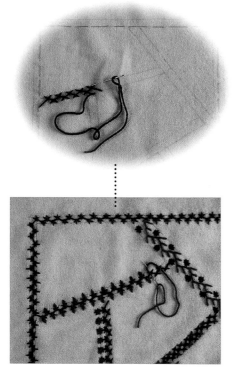

3 Using one strand of tapestry wool and a tapestry needle, begin working a combination stitch along one of the "patches" between the parallel lines (or using the lines as a guide for the base stitch). Work the second journey of the stitch in the contrasting color. Continue in this way, using a different stitch for each line in the block, but using the same stitch along the outer edge of the block. (See opposite page and pages 112 and 113 for combination stitches.)

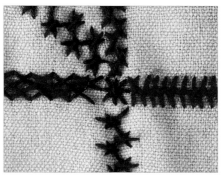

4 After the first block has been completed, embroider the second block, continuing to use the same stitch around the outer edge of the blocks throughout. Then draw the random patch lines in the remaining blocks; either use the same two or three random patch layouts, just turning them for variety, or draw a completely different arrangement in each block. At the block corners (except those along the outer edge), work a star stitch (see above).

5 When the embroidery has been completed, turn ¹/₂in (1.5cm) to the wrong side around the edge of the throw and baste. Then using a water soluble pen, draw a line ¹/₂in (1.5cm) from the fold as a guide for the edging embroidery. Work crossed buttonhole stitch (see page 109) around the edge, changing the color of thread as desired. Remove the basting and the pen marks, and steam press the throw lightly on the wrong side over a padded surface.

COMBINATION-STITCH ALTERNATIVES

CRAZY PATCHWORK HAS traditionally used combination stitches to lavishly embellish patch edges. These stitches look elaborate but are usually made up of two or three simple embroidery stitches worked side-by-side or interlinked. The stitches can be worked in a single thread color or in a different color for each stitch, whatever suits your crazy-patchwork design and color scheme.

Once the principle of combination stitches is understood any number of combinations can be created. There are nine combination stitches given in the Stitch Library on pages 112 and 113, and some more are illustrated here. Don't hesitate to make up your own alternative combinations; all the simple stitches to choose from are given on pages 108–111.

These three tips for working combination stitches might come in handy. First of all, you might find it easier to work the stitches with the fabric mounted in an embroidery hoop.

Just move the hoop after each area is completed. Secondly, be sure to draw parallel guidelines for the stitches using a water soluble pen; the marks are removable. Thirdly, work the stitches in the recommended or logical order.

BELOW *If desired, use this alternative colorway—a royal blue ground and red and white threads—for your wool throw. Each stitch is worked in the order the individual stitches are listed. On the left from top to bottom: feather and star stitches; herringbone and lazy daisy stitches; herringbone, and star stitch with an elongated arm; cretan and lazy daisy stitches; petal stitch, lazy daisy, and French knots; French knots. In the center: cretan stitch and French knots. On the right from top to bottom: feather stitch, lazy daisy, and French knots; herringbone, lazy daisy, and straight stitches; buttonhole fans and French knots; cretan and straight stitches; feather and lazy daisy stitches.*

ROMANTIC COLLECTION

*Crazy patchwork can make enchanting
and romantic mementos, especially when
worked in sweet pastels and florals and
dotted with delicate embroideries.*

THE DESIGNS IN the Romantic Collection are all worked in cheerful candy-colored pastels, with an emphasis on dainty floral prints, sunny plaids, and exquisite silks. Each of the motley crazy patch arrangements features a different embellishment, be it gilding, beads, cross-stitch, floral appliqué, or ribbon embroidery.

The projects include a patchwork picture, a stuffed heart, a baby blanket, a box, and a cushion. With their embroidered monograms, dates, and messages, and the clever inclusion of treasured antique embroidered scraps, they serve as reminders of the wonderful commemorative crazy quilts of the nineteenth century. What better way to commemorate a cherished event—a birth, a marriage, or an anniversary—than to stitch precious memories into a crazy patchwork!

An alternative design is given with each of the items in this chapter, offering an easier-to-work, though just as enchanting option. A dedicated crazy patchworker might be inspired to turn one of these romantic concoctions into a full-sized quilt.

CROSS-STITCH BABY QUILT

Crazy patchwork made up of pretty romantic prints is especially suited to baby accessories. This handsome padded quilt cleverly combines three patchwork panels and two aida bands with bold cross-stitch embroidery.

THE LIGHTWEIGHT cotton fabrics used for this design are mostly small-scale prints, and some checks, all manufactured especially for patchwork. Seasoned patchworkers will only have to rummage around in their remnant chest to find just the right selection of the sweet, pastel-toned prints. But if the right combination is not at hand, the scraps could be obtained from quilt shops in bags filled with a variety of complementary swatches. Or, old children's dresses in tiny prints could be conveniently recycled.

To tie the theme of the cross-stitched aida bands on this quilt into the crazy patchwork, colored even-

weave aida with embroidered motifs has been used for a few of the patches in each of the three panels. The aida patch colors—creams and pastels—and the embroidery threads were carefully chosen to tone in with the prints.

LEFT *This quilt is edged with a simple ruffle and padded with quilt batting. It is tied together at random patch corners and measures 26in (66cm) by 40in (100cm), excluding the ruffle.*

RIGHT *Working cross-stitches on aida is a very easy technique. And because the stitches on this quilt are worked over two aida squares in each direction, the embroidery is also surprisingly quick.*

MATERIALS FOR THE QUILT

ABOVE

A selection of the crazy-patch prints, aida fabrics, and embroidery threads used on the baby quilt.

You will need

- **Crazy-patch scraps** ~ lightweight cotton in pale, pretty, romantic small-scale prints and checks
- **14-count aida** ~ two 2in (5cm) wide white bands 27½in (70cm) long, and nine 6in (15cm) pastel squares
- **Foundation fabric** ~ neutral-colored cotton fabric
- **Sewing threads** ~ basting thread, invisible monofilament thread, and matching sewing thread
- **Embroidery thread** ~ at least eight to nine shades of stranded cotton embroidery floss
- **Ruffle** ~ 1½yd (1.3m) of a small-scale check 44in (112cm) wide
- **Batting** ~ same size as quilt front
- **Quilt backing** ~ 1yd (1m) of a small-scale print 44in (112cm) wide

MAKING THE QUILT PATCHWORK

THE WORD BABY in different languages adorns the two aida-band panels on the Cross-stitch Baby Quilt. You can personalize the quilt by embroidering the baby's name and birth date, or even part of a poem, on the bands instead. Charted cross-stitch letters, numerals, and motifs are provided in the Stitch Glossary on pages 114–116.

 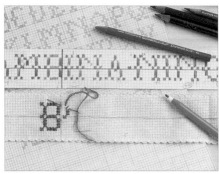 

1 Before beginning the patchwork, cross-stitch the animal motifs onto the nine squares of evenweave aida (see page 114 for the motif charts). Fold the aida in half both lengthwise and width-wise and mark the center. Mount the aida in a hoop. Using six strands of floss and a tapestry needle, stitch the animal motif from the center outward, working each cross-stitch over two aida squares in each direction. Set the finished squares aside to use later.

2 Next, decide on the message you want to embroider across the two aida-band panels. Chart the message on graph paper using the cross-stitch alphabet on page 114. Note that 26in (66cm) of the aida band will accommo-date about 182 cross-stitches (worked over two-by-two aida squares) along the length and about 9 or 10 stitches across the depth. Work the cross-stitches as for the motifs. Start stitching at the center of the aida and work outward.

3 Cut three pieces of foundation fabric for the patchwork panels, each measuring 27^1/$_2$in (70cm) by 13^1/$_2$in (34cm) including the ^{3}/$_4$in (2cm) seam allowance. To make the crazy patchwork, position three stitched aida patches in place inside each panel and piece the fabric print patches around them. As you proceed, fold under the edges of the patches, baste in place, then machine zigzag using invisible thread (see pages 22 and 23 for techniques).

4 Once the crazy patchwork has been completed on each of the three foundation panels, decorate the patch seams. Using six strands of embroidery floss and a pointed needle, embroider the patch seams with herringbone stitch. For an especially colorful effect, use a different color of thread for each side of the patch.

5 Mark the center of the aida bands and patchwork panels with basted lines. Matching the marked lines, baste the aida bands and the panels together.

PATCHWORK ALTERNATIVES

Hopefully the Cross-stitch Baby Quilt will inspire you to look for other fabric and color themes for crazy-patch baby quilts. The alternative idea suggested here is a stunning patchwork made of lace and *broderie anglaise*.

6 Using invisible monofilament thread, machine zigzag the four basted seams. Then using six strands of embroidery floss and a pointed needle, embroider these seams with herringbone stitch as shown above. For a multicolored line of herringbone, change the thread color as each needlefull is used up. Then remove the basting. Attach the backing and the batting, tie the layers together, and edge the quilt with a ruffle as explained on page 124.

Tying a crazy-patch quilt

Because the embroidery on crazy patchwork should not be covered with lines of quilting, it is best to join the quilt front, batting, and backing with ties instead. Multicolored ties blend in nicely with any design (see below).

ABOVE *This alternative crazy patchwork baby quilt is made of antique pieces of handmade* broderie anglaise, *cutwork, hand and machine lace, and crochet, all arranged and stitched onto a pale-colored cotton foundation fabric.*

Lace crazy patches are much easier to stitch than might be expected. The highly flexible raw edges of the lace need not be turned under, but instead the finished self-edges of some lace patches can be overlapped over the cut raw edges of

others. The lace patches are basted to the foundation one by one and then machine zigzagged with invisible monofilament thread (see page 22).

If you want to make a crazy quilt like this and don't have or can't find enough antique pieces to use, your scraps can be supplemented with remnants of present-day machine-made broderie anglaise *and lace. Mixed together carefully the antique and contemporary crazy patches should blend in perfectly.*

GILDED PICTURE

The metal-leaf motifs on this striking crazy-patch picture are easily applied

to the silk scraps with fusible web adhesive. Once gilded, the patches are pieced together and

then edged with shiny gold and silver embroidery threads.

ALTHOUGH GILDED silk scraps are not ideal for items that need to be hardwearing, they are excellent for making ornamental crazy-patchwork frames, boxes, or stuffed hearts (see pages 94, 76, and 72). The combination of metal leaf, silks, and gold and silver embroidery threads creates a lush and precious surface just right for a memento of a special event.

Scraps in different textures—raw silk, lining silk, and silk satin—have been included in this design to give it subtly effective variety. The slubbed

and smooth silks also alter the effects of the gilding. The flat surfaces make the gilding appear extra shiny and the bumpy ones make it crack into an interesting antiqued texture.

LEFT *The completed Gilded Picture measures 9¹/₂in (24cm) by 12in (30cm).*
RIGHT *The gilded motifs are all symbols of love and fidelity, making the picture a good gift for a marriage, a wedding anniversary, or Valentine's day. For an extra-special event, substitute real gold or silver leaf for the metal leaf used here.*

MATERIALS FOR THE PICTURE

ABOVE *A selection of the silk crazy-patch fabrics, metallic embroidery threads, and metal leaf used on the Gilded Picture.*

You will need

- **Crazy-patch scraps** ~ a range of plain silks in sweet pastels
- **Foundation fabric** ~ lightweight cotton
- **Sewing threads** ~ basting thread and invisible monofilament thread
- **Embroidery thread** ~ gold, silver, and bronze metallic embroidery threads
- **Fusible web** ~ paper-backed fusible web, for attaching metal leaf
- **Gold and silver leaf** ~ artificial gold and silver metal leaf, for gilding patches
- **Special tool** ~ acrylic paint brush (or old soft toothbrush) for gilding technique
- **Picture mount** ~ piece of ¹/₄in (6mm) thick art board with a polystyrene core 9¹/₂in (24cm) by 12in (30cm)
- **Padding** ~ piece of polyester batting same size as cardboard picture mount
- **Backing** ~ piece of lightweight silk 11¹/₂in (29cm) by 14in (35cm)
- **Trim** ~ narrow velvet ribbon
- **Fabric glue** ~ for mounting

MAKING THE PICTURE PATCHWORK

W HEN PLANNING YOUR crazy-patch gilded picture, first decide on the size and type of monogram. The monogram used for the picture shown here was taken from the alphabet on page 117, but you might want to design your own letters or even make a gilded monogram instead (see the tip box on the opposite page). A larger monogram might necessitate a larger picture mount than the size given in the materials list, so if necessary alter the size of the art board before beginning the crazy patchwork.

The gilding technique is quite easy to master, but if in doubt, practice it with a tiny motif on a piece of scrap cotton before working directly onto your precious silks.

1 Before beginning the patchwork, decorate the patches with gilded motifs. Trace a motif onto the paper side of a piece of paper-backed fusible web and cut out the shape (see page 117 for motifs). Then place the glue side of the fusible-web motif on the right side of a patch and press in place following the manufacturer's instructions.

2 Remove the paper backing from the web. Then lay the metal leaf on top of the fusible-web on the patch and place a piece of paper on top of the metal leaf (you can use the paper that comes between the sheets of metal leaf). Keeping the paper in place over the leaf and using a moderately hot iron, press the metal leaf onto the fusible web.

3 Remove the paper on top of the metal leaf. Then using a dry paint brush, gently brush away the surplus leaf around the edge of the shape and inside the shape as well. Prepare the remaining patches in the same way. If you are unsure how many patches you will need, prepare about ten patches first, then prepare more as you proceed.

4 For the central monogram, choose a silk patch large enough to mount on an embroidery hoop (the excess can be trimmed away later if necessary). Then gild a large heart onto the patch. Mount the gilded patch in a hoop and work a trammed satin stitch monogram in the center of the patch over the heart motif, using a single strand of gold or silver metallic embroidery thread. (See page 117 for an alphabet for satin stitch letters and page 33 for how to work trammed satin stitch.)

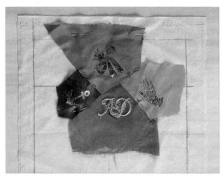

5 Using a water soluble pen and the picture mount, trace the picture outline onto the foundation fabric. Then draw a second line 1in (2.5cm) outside the outline for the seam allowance. Pin the monogram patch to the foundation, positioning it in the center of the picture and about 4$^{1}/_{2}$in (11.5cm) from the top. Begin piecing the patches around this focal patch, overlapping them by about $^{1}/_{4}$in (6mm). Pin, baste, and machine zigzag the patches using invisible thread (see page 22 for this technique).

6 After all the patches have been secured with machine zigzag, cover the raw edges between the patches with hand embroidery to hide the monofilament stitches. Using as many strands of metallic embroidery thread as needed for a bold effect, work herringbone stitch over the joins (see page 111 for how to work herringbone stitch). For variety, use a different gold or silver thread for each side of a patch. This will give the surface decoration a much more lively appearance.

7 Once all the the joins between the patches have been embroidered, trim the outer edge of the patchwork to to straighten it if necessary. Try to leave a generous amount of extra fabric around the edge of your picture. This extra fabric can then be turned to the back of the picture mount and glued to the back. If, however, the motifs have been positioned too near the edge of the patchwork, the narrow border around the edge can be glued to the side edge (instead of the back) of a thick picture mount and the edge covered with a ribbon. Turn to page 122 for instructions on how to attach the completed crazy patchwork to the padded mount.

Gilded monograms

Working a trammed satin stitch monogram for your picture requires a certain amount of skill, so you might want to make a gilded monogram instead. Just trace the letters onto the fusible paper-backed web, cut them out, bond to the patch, and gild as for other motifs.

PATCHWORK ALTERNATIVES

THE GILDED Picture was designed with a romantic celebration in mind, but it could easily be altered to suit another event merely by changing the motifs; for instance, flower motifs for mother's day or little birds and bunnies for a birth. Also—instead of a monogram—a message, date, or name could be embroidered on the central patch. If gilded silk patches and gold and silver embroidery threads are too extravagant for the occasion, plain and printed cottons could be used for the patches, and simple ribbons, braids, or rickrack for the seam decoration.

RIGHT *To make this alternative picture personal, the child's name has been embroidered over the handwriting of the giver—in this case her grandmother. Also, some of the fabrics used are from dresses made for her by her grandmother. To make the patchwork, first work the embroidery onto a few scraps, using stranded floss (see page 119 for motifs, and page 33 for how to embroider signatures). Then machine zigzag the pieces onto the foundation and cover the joins with rickrack in various shades.*

RIBBON-EMBROIDERED CUSHION

Embroidered and appliquéd scraps cut from secondhand linens are used to

make this cushion cover. The crazy-patch edges are covered with herringbone and feather

stitches worked in fine, brightly colored embroidery ribbon.

THERE IS NO NEED to embroider or appliqué your own patches for this cushion cover. Either your own linen drawer or local flea markets, thrift shops, and rummage sales will harbor plenty of willing candidates. Table cloths, tray cloths, place mats, guest hand towels, and napkins with this type of sweetly colored embroidery and appliqué were made in abundance in the 1940's and 1950's. Comparable linens are still made in China today.

Friends, relatives, and neighbors may even agree to contribute treasured, but long unused embroidered and appliquéd

linens to your scrap collection when they realize they are going into an even more beautiful arrangement of crazy patches!

LEFT *Trimming away most of the white ground fabric around the embroidery or appliqué keeps the overall cushion-cover design colorful and lively. The bright, bold ribbon embroidery emphasizes the joins between the patches.*
RIGHT *Generous in size, the finished cushion measures 19in (48cm) square. If your collection of scraps is extensive, make a matching pair of cushions.*

MATERIALS FOR THE CUSHION

ABOVE *A selection of the embroidery ribbons and the secondhand embroidered and appliquéd linen crazy-patch fabrics used on the Ribbon-embroidered Cushion.*

You will need

- **Crazy-patch scraps** ~ patches cut from secondhand linen (see above for finding scraps) with embroidery and/or appliqué in candy colors
- **Foundation fabric** ~ white lightweight cotton fabric, for patches base
- **Sewing threads** ~ basting thread, invisible monofilament thread, and matching thread for backing
- **Embroidery ribbon** ~ silk (or rayon) embroidery ribbons in different widths and a range of colors that matches appliqué and embroidery on scraps
- **Border strips** ~ four 4in (10cm) wide white linen or cotton strips, two 16in (41cm) long and two 23in (55cm) long
- **Cushion cover back** ~ piece of white linen or cotton fabric
- **Pillow form** ~ to fit cushion cover
- **Fasteners** ~ snaps or zipper for cushion cover opening (optional)

MAKING THE CUSHION PATCHWORK

THE PATCHES ON this cushion cover are machine zigzagged in place with invisible monofilament thread, and the patch joins are covered with ribbon embroidery. The light-weight silk and rayon ribbons designed especially for ribbon embroidery are fine enough to pass through a large long-eyed embroidery needle.

The needle should be thick enough to create a hole in the fabric large enough for the ribbon to pass easily through behind it. Unless you are an accomplished ribbon embroiderer, it is probably best to stretch the patchwork onto an embroidery hoop to work the stitches. To avoid the ribbon end slipping out of the needle eye, you can pass the tip of the needle through the ribbon 1/4in (6mm) from the end; this locks the needle in place. While embroidering, flatten the ribbon with the needle tip after each stitch is made.

1 Using a water soluble pen and a ruler, draw a 15in (38cm) square onto the foundation fabric. Then add an extra 3/4in (2cm) all around the for seam allowance and cut out the square. Cutting the scraps with a generous amount of ground fabric left around the embroidery or appliqué, begin arranging the patches at one corner. Trim the patch edges to fit together and so that they overlap by about 1/4in (6mm). Pin the patches in place as they are trimmed, then baste the raw edges.

2 After basting the patches, secure them with machine stitches. Thread the sewing machine with invisible mono-filament thread (see page 22 for more about monofilament thread). Then machine zigzag the raw patch edges (see page 22 for detailed instructions for this method of piecing crazy patches). Continue in this way, basting and machine stitching patches in place, until the entire foundation fabric is covered with patches, including the seam allowance. Remove the basting threads.

3 After all the patches have been zigzagged in place, decorate the joins between the patches with ribbon embroidery. Thread the needle with a length of ribbon in a color that complements the patch decoration, then work along one side of the patch in herringbone stitch covering the zigzagged raw edges. Continue in this way, but altering both the stitch and the ribbon color at random for variety.

4 Press the completed patchwork very lightly on the wrong side over a padded surface. Trim the patchwork into a 16in (41cm) square. With right sides facing and taking a 1/2in (1.5cm) seam allowance, machine stitch one short border strip to each of two opposite sides of the patchwork using a matching thread. Press the seams open. Stitch the longer border strips to the remaining sides of the patchwork in the same way and press the seams open. Baste lengths of embroidery ribbons over the seams between the patchwork and the border, crossing the ribbons at the corners as shown above.

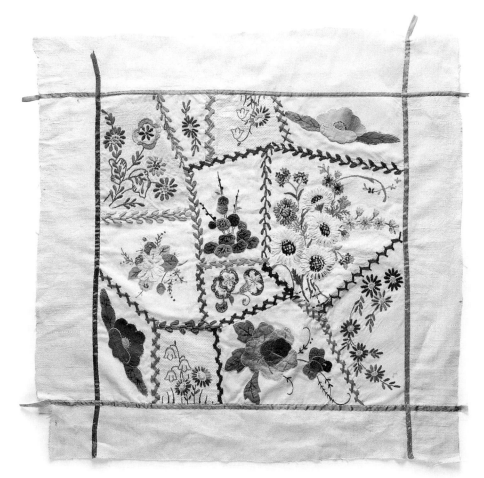

5 When basting the embroidery ribbons to the seams between the patchwork and the borders, use a different colored embroidery ribbon for each of the seams as shown on the left. After the ribbons have been basted in position over the seams, machine stitch them in place. To do this, first thread the sewing machine (and the bobbin) with monofilament thread. Then machine zigzag stitch the ribbons in place, stitching down first one side of the ribbon, then the other side. Next, remove the basting threads that were used to secure the ribbons in place. Now trim the completed piece to approximately 20in (51cm) by 20in (51cm), ensuring the each of the border strips is the same width. This trimmed size will leave a $1/2$in (1.5cm) seam allowance around the edge of the cushion cover front. To complete the cushion, turn to page 122 for instructions on backing the cushion.

PATCHWORK ALTERNATIVES

ALTHOUGH RIBBON embroidery creates a bold effect on crazy patchwork, it is slower to work with than ordinary embroidery threads. So if you are looking for an alternative embellishment for your cushion cover, embroidery worked in stranded cotton or silk floss would be a good option. Another advantage of floss is that it will pass more easily through closely woven grounds (such as pillowcases) than ribbon will. The ultimate alternative to the Ribbon-Embroidered Cushion, would be to use patches that you have embroidered yourself instead of using secondhand embroideries!

RIGHT *Stranded embroidery floss has been used here for seam decoration instead of silk embroidery ribbon. Close cropping of the ground fabric around the embroideries and the use of multicolored combination embroidery stitches creates an intensely ornate and busy surface.*

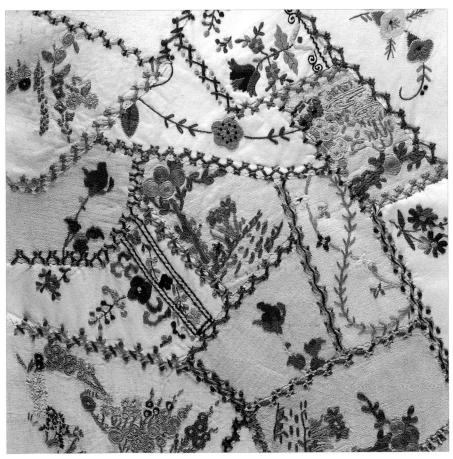

BEADED HEART

The small ribbon and fabric scraps on this commemorative crazy patchwork are pinned directly onto the stuffed felt heart. The only sewing involved is the machine and hand stitching used to make the heart itself.

MAKING A decorated stuffed heart from your most precious scraps is a wonderful way to commemorate a celebration. The unique pinning technique used to secure the patches on this design is a quick method of composing crazy patchwork and is especially suited to tiny scraps that would be difficult to stitch. The beads and sequins are slipped onto the lace pins before the pins are inserted through the patch edges. Although lace pins are quite fine, they will not pass through some beads, so the smallest beads should be tested before purchase. Big beads with holes too large for the pin heads are not a problem, since they can be used in conjunction with a tiny bead that is slipped onto the pin first.

LEFT *The heart measures about 8in (20cm) across from top to tip and about 8¹/₂in (22cm) across the widest part.*
RIGHT *Encrusted with glittering beads and sequins, this heart patchwork is made up of tiny scraps of precious antique and modern ribbons and a few plain silks.*

MATERIALS FOR THE HEART

You will need

- **Crazy-patch scraps** ~ an assortment of embroidered, plain, plaid, and ruffled ribbons, and plain silks, in pastels
- **Heart fabric** ~ piece of felt 12in (30cm) by 24in (61cm) for making stuffed heart
- **Stuffing** ~ sawdust (from pet store) for stuffing felt heart
- **Backing** ~ piece of silk 12in (30cm) by 12in (30cm) for covering back of heart
- **Sewing threads** ~ matching threads for sewing felt heart and attaching backing fabric
- **Special material** ~ tissue paper
- **Pins** ~ gold- or silver-colored tarnish-proof lace pins
- **Beads and sequins** ~ an assortment of tiny, medium-sized, and large round glass beads in colors that complement patches, and flat silver 5mm sequins
- **Ribbon** ~ length of ¹/₄in (6mm) wide velvet ribbon, for edging heart

ABOVE
A selection of the precious scrap fabrics stitched into the Beaded Heart, including textured, embroidered, plain, and patterned ribbons, and plain silks. Also, the beads and sequins used to pin the patches onto the stuffed heart, and the velvet ribbon seam trim.

M A K I N G T H E H E A R T P A T C H W O R K

R IBBONS ARE AN important source of scraps for tiny patches. Folding under the raw edges of small patches is intricate work, especially on silks that fray easily and are more difficult to crease than cottons. The selvages on ribbons eliminate the need for hems and can be lapped over other raw edges. If ribbons scraps are not included in the selection of silks for this heart, the individual scraps can be backed with a fine fusible interfacing before being cut and pieced. Placing the sequins together so that they touch, hide the raw edges. A template for the stuffed heart and instructions for making it are given at the back of the book. An alphabet and numerals are also provided for the letters and dates.

1 First, make the felt stuffed heart (see page 123). Then using the template on page 119, cut out the silk backing on the bias. Clipping the seam allowance as necessary, pin the backing to one side of the heart. Stitch in place, inserting the needle through the backing and the felt seam allowance. Trim the seam.

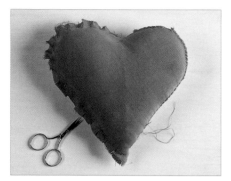

2 Begin your patchwork by planning the letters and the date. Design your own alphabet and numerals, or use those given on page 117. Trace the two desired letters onto separate pieces of tissue paper using a pencil. Then trace the date onto a third piece of tissue paper carefully aligning the numbers.

3 Place plain patches in the desired positions on the heart for the two letters and the date, and pin temporarily in position. Lay the tracing paper letters on top of each of the patches and fill in the shapes by pinning on tiny beads. When the letters are completely beaded, gently pull away the tissue paper.

4 Begin arranging the patches around the beaded letters, trimming them to fit and overlapping the edges about ¼in (6mm). Secure the corners of the patches with temporary pins and begin covering the joins between the patches with beads and sequins; onto each pin slide a bead, then a sequin. (When using beads with a large hole, slip an extra tiny bead onto the pin first.) Insert the tips of the pins close to the edge of the patches. Replace all the temporary corner pins with large matching beads. This will give unity to the design.

5 Continuing in this way, add more patches, changing the colors of the beads on each side of each patch and placing the sequins close together to hide the patch joins. Before pinning the scraps around the date patch, add the date as for the letters, pinning on tiny beads over the thick sections of the numbers and only pins over thin sections. Then attach the remaining patches, ensuring that the outer patches cover the stuffed heart seam. Next, pin the patches along the heart seam line and trim the edges close to the seam line.

6 Place one end of the narrow velvet ribbon ¼in (6mm) to the right of the center top of the heart over the raw edge of the patch, and pin temporarily. Then slide a small bead onto a pin and insert the pin through the ribbon about ½in (12mm) to the left of the heart center. Continue pinning the ribbon over the raw patch edges, using alternately a small and large bead on the pin and a small bead only. When the center top of the heart is reached, fold under the end of the ribbon and pin it to the center position with a small and large bead.

PATCHWORK ALTERNATIVES

ALTERNATIVE designs for stuffed hearts will depend on the event you are commemorating or on the recepient of the gift. While extravagant decorations and priceless patches are good for adult keepsakes, less ornate ingredients might be better for a get-well heart or a child's birthday (see the Gingham Heart on page 51, which uses crisp cottons instead of silks.) Also, wooden or metal beads could be used in place of glass beads.

BELOW *This patchwork was designed for a wedding heart from luxurious white laces and machine-embroidered silks. The patch edges have been folded under and secured with round and flower-shaped pearl beads and white glass beads.*

APPLIQUÉD BOX

Pieced together from floral, striped, and plaid scarves and handkerchiefs,

this crazy-patch box cover is decorated with a few appliqué motifs. The patch joins are

covered with a bold decorative machine zigzag stitch.

O NE OF THE JOYS of crazy patch-work is being able to make use of beautiful fabrics that have lost their use as garments. The stacks of multi-colored scarves and handkerchiefs at the bottom of a drawer, although long unused, are sure to still be a treat to the eye. Rummage sales and thrift shops also often have boxes full of these little cotton, rayon, and silk treasures. Special scarves and handkerchiefs seem to be kept and sold on because the owners recognize the exceptional quality of their vibrant dyes and elaborate plaids,

stripes, and floral prints. The addition of bonded floral appliqué motifs and the occasional piece of embroidered ribbon, introduces a little texture into the otherwise smooth surface of this design.

LEFT *The focal color theme of the Appliquéd Box is one of strong contrasts. Vibrant stripes and plaids are interspersed among soft pastel flowers on white, black, or high pastel grounds.*

RIGHT *The patchwork can be made to fit any size box, but the box pictured is 11in (28cm) square and 4¹⁄₄in (11cm) deep.*

MATERIALS FOR THE BOX

ABOVE *A selection of the silk, rayon, and cotton handkerchiefs and scarves, floral print patch fabrics, embroidered ribbons, and machine embroidery threads used on the Appliquéd Box.*

You will need

- **Crazy-patch scraps** ~ plain, floral print, and striped silk, rayon, and cotton scarves and hankies, and embroidered ribbon scraps, all in strong colors
- **Foundation fabric** ~ lightweight white cotton fabric
- **Sewing thread** ~ basting thread and invisible monofilament thread
- **Appliqué motifs** ~ cut from floral prints
- **Fusible web** ~ paper-backed fusible web for bonding appliqué to patches
- **Embroidery thread** ~ silk buttonhole thread for machine embroidery, in a range of complementary colors
- **Box** ~ neutral-colored square cardboard box with lid
- **Lid trim** ~ velvet ribbon same width as depth of box lid, for covering lid lip
- **Box base trim** ~ fine ribbon same depth as lid, for top of crazy patch-work piece on box base
- **Fabric glue** ~ for finishing box

MAKING THE BOX PATCHWORK

SELECT SCARVES and handkerchiefs for your crazy patchwork that are fairly lightweight, but not transparent. Heavyweight fabrics will not work well on a box patchwork, since they will be too thick for the lid to fit over. Keep this in mind when choosing embroidered ribbon scraps to sprinkle into the patch arrangement.

Cut the fabrics into rough patch shapes as you go. Do not cut off the finely hemmed or rolled edges on the scarf and handkerchief scraps, or the selvage on the ribbon scraps. When piecing the patches, use these finished edges as a design feature and to conceal the raw edges of adjacent patches.

If desired, fuse a few floral appliqué motifs onto the finished patchwork over awkward patch corners. Then machine zigzag the edge of the motif with invisible monofilament thread.

1 Before beginning the patchwork, apply appliqué motifs chosen from the floral print scraps onto a few of the patches. First, bond fusible web onto the back of the motif. Then cut the motif out, remove the paper backing, and bond the appliqué onto a solid-colored patch. Lastly, machine zigzag the motif edge with monofilament thread (see page 31 for more about appliqué). Appliqué flowers onto a few patches to use for the base patchwork.

2 Next, prepare the patchwork foundation fabric by marking the outline of the top of the lid onto it using a water soluble pen. Add an extra 3/4in (2cm) all around for the seam allowance, which will be glued to the lid lip. (The patchwork only covers the lid top; the lip of the lid will be covered later with ribbon.) Starting at one corner of the foundation, pin and baste the patches in place overlapping the raw patch edges by about 1/8in (3mm).

3 Once the patches have been basted in place, decorate the joins between the patches with machine embroidery. Using a large-eyed jeans needle and silk buttonhole thread, work machine embroidery over the raw edges, with the machine set for a wide, close zigzag.

4 Continue in this way, working machine embroidery over the patch seams and changing the color of thread on each side of each patch. When the foundation fabric, including the seam allowance, has been covered with patches and the machine embroidery has been completed, trim the edges to straighten if necessary.

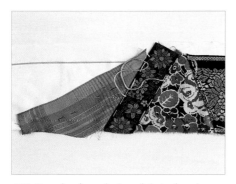

Embroidered appliqué

Instead of cutting flower motifs from floral print scraps for your appliqué motifs, you can cut machine-embroidered flowers from embroidered ribbons, or hand-embroidered flowers from second-hand embroideries. Just bond fusible web to the back of the motif, cut out, and apply as for ordinary appliqué.

5 For the foundation fabric for the box base, cut a rectangle as long as the circumference of the base plus an extra 1in (2.5cm) for the overlap, and exactly as wide as the box depth. Mark a line across the top of the fabric as far from the raw edge as the box lid depth. Piece the patches in place as for the lid patchwork, overlapping the lid line by ¼in (6mm) and extending the patchwork past the foundation fabric at the lower edge by ¼in (6mm).

6 Machine embroider the patch edges as for the lid patchwork. Then fold the ¼in (6mm) patchwork overlap at the lower edge to the wrong side and machine embroider along the fold. Baste on the fine ribbon, aligning the top edges of the ribbon and foundation. Machine embroider along the join between the ribbon and patchwork. Trim away the foundation and patchwork under the ribbon. Turn to page 125 for how to attach the patchwork to the box.

PATCHWORK ALTERNATIVES

Y OUR COLLECTION of scarves and handkerchiefs will probably not match the shades of those on the Appliqué Box, so base your color theme around what you have at hand. Arrange your crazy-patch scraps by trial and error and notice the different effect achieved when the scraps with white or black grounds are eliminated and just those with pastel grounds are included. The Ribbon Box on page 91 shows another example of an alternative patchwork for a box cover. Wide ribbons in pastel tones and sweet florals could be used instead to fit the Romantic theme of this chapter.

RIGHT *This striking design is made in the same way as the Appliqué Box patchwork, but uses ready-made embroidered appliqués. The color scheme is also very different—strong solid yellows predominate and are punctuated with a few other high pastel tones and sharply contrasting floral prints with black grounds.*

ANTIQUE COLLECTION

The patchworks in this collection were inspired by the rich colors, sumptuous fabrics, lavish embroidery, and fine trims that are the hallmarks of traditional crazy quilts.

T HE ALMOST theatrical quality of traditional crazy patchwork housed in museums is an inspiration even today. Drawn from this tradition, the designs in the Antique Collection are composed of rich mosaics in a broad range of fabrics that includes brocades, velvets, tartans, chenilles, fine wools, paisleys, silks, and even metallic laces. Braids, fringes, ribbons, beads, tassels, and hand- and machine-embroidered seams and motifs, provide the ornate surface embellishments.

The items in this collection—a lampshade, cushion, frame, box, bag, and scarf—are all relatively quick to make. The lampshade and cushion would both be excellent projects for a crazy-patchwork novice.

Each of the designs presents a unique and attractive combination of color, fabric, and trim. For those who would like to produce a lasting heirloom, any of these crazy-patch creations, or the accompanying alternative designs, could quite easily be used as the basis for a stunning quilt.

EMBROIDERED LAMPSHADE

Used to decorate a lampshade, crazy patchwork takes on the

delightful attributes of stained glass. The patch color scheme looks rich and sedate when the light

is switched off and glows when it is switched on.

THIS LAMPSHADE project is one of the quickest patchworks to make in the book. But a little extra time should be taken in the planning stages to carefully choose fabrics and secondhand embroideries. At least a small selection of the scraps should be transparent enough to allow some light through, so that the design will take on the look of stained glass.

To test your fabrics for transparency, first mount the lampshade on the lamp stand and switch on the light. Then drape the scraps one at a time over the lamp-shade to see what they will look like when illuminated from behind. If you are using any opaque patches, make sure that you sprinkle them evenly among the others in the final crazy-patch arrangement.

LEFT *Opaque and semi-transparent fabrics can be used effectively for lampshade crazy patchworks. This lampshade uses a combination of all three. The alternative colorway on page 85 uses paler and more see-through fabrics.*

RIGHT *When choosing fabrics and trims for your lampshade, pick colors that will complement your interior, yet make a subtle statement of their own. There is no need to restrict your lampshade to the size of those shown here, and even the shape is up to you. Any lampshade with a simple, flat cone- or tube-shape is quite easy to cover, since it will require only a single piece of crazy patchwork. The step-by-step directions on page 84 explain how to copy the lampshade shape onto a large piece of paper.*

MATERIALS FOR THE LAMPSHADE

BELOW *A selection of the crazy-patch fabrics, secondhand embroideries, and embroidery threads used on the Embroidered Lampshade.*

You will need

- **Crazy-patch scraps** ~ solids, brocades, stripes, plaids, velvets, and paisleys, all in rich antique shades
- **Embroidered scraps** ~ three or four scraps of secondhand embroidery (optional highlights)
- **Foundation fabric** ~ lightweight fusible woven white interfacing
- **Sewing thread** ~ basting thread and invisible monofilament thread
- **Embroidery thread** ~ pearl cotton in a variety of colors
- **Trim** ~ cord or braid for decorating lower edge of lampshade
- **Lampshade** ~ made from stiff card-board, in white or cream
- **Fabric glue** ~ for attaching completed patchwork to lampshade

MAKING THE LAMPSHADE PATCHWORK

BEFORE BEGINNING the crazy-patchwork lampshade, make a careful selection of the fabrics as described and illustrated on page 82. Ensure that you have a large enough variety of prints and colors among the scraps to make an interesting layout of random patch shapes. When trimming and overlapping the patches make sure that they overlap only slightly and that the overlap is even. The overlap will be covered by embroidery later, but if any excess fabric extends past the embroidery stitches underneath, it will show through the thinner patches when the light is turned on.

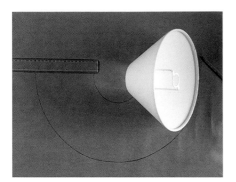

1 To begin the lampshade template, draw a straight line on a large piece of paper. Align the lampshade seam line with the straight line; then slowly rolling the lampshade, draw the top and lower edges until you reach the starting point. Remove the lampshade and draw a straight line between the top and lower edges. Cut out the template.

2 To prepare the foundation for the patches, trace the lampshade shape onto the glue side of the fusible interfacing, using the template. Cut out, adding an extra 1in (2.5cm) all around for the seam allowance. Then starting at one corner, fuse a few patches in place so that they are very slightly overlapping (see above and page 22).

3 Once a few patches are bonded in place, machine zigzag stitch them to the foundation interfacing using invisible monofilament thread. Making sure that the patches are covering the seam allowance, continue in this way, bonding then stitching a few patches at a time until the crazy patchwork covers the entire foundation piece.

4 Once all the patches have been secured to the foundation, thread an embroidery needle with pearl cotton and work herringbone stitch over the raw edges of the patches. Change the thread color for each line of stitches so that each side of each patch is decorated with a different color. Place the finished patchwork piece face down on a padded surface and press with a warm iron. (See page 24 for more information on decorating crazy-patch seams with embroidery, and page 111 for how to work herringbone stitch.)

5 Bonding and stitching the crazy patches onto the foundation fabric may have caused the shape of the crazy patchwork to shrink slightly, so it is important to retrace the original lampshade shape onto it. Place the finished and pressed patchwork face down on a flat surface. Then using the original paper template (see Step 1) and a water soluble pen, trace the lampshade shape onto the wrong side of the patchwork. If necessary, trim the seam allowance around the edge of the traced outline to 3/4in (2cm). Turn to page 125 for how to join the patchwork seam to form it into a cone shape and for how to attach the patchwork to the lampshade.

PATCHWORK ALTERNATIVES

CRAZY PATCHWORK can be very effective when used on items where the light will shine through it, such as lampshades, room screens, and window blinds. If the patchwork will be seen on both sides, as it would on a screen or blind, a net or scrim could be used for the foundation.

BELOW *If you are looking for an alternative colorway for your lampshade, try fabrics in a range of lighter tones and mix them with bits of lace. This combination will let more light through and give a fresher atmosphere to your room than the darker, more dramatic hues used on page 83.*

BRAIDED CUSHION

Sumptuous and rich in appearance, this cushion took just four hours to stitch.

The patches were joined with the simple bonding technique, and decorative braids and

ribbons were machine stitched over the crazy-patch joins.

THE LARGE ANGULAR crazy patches on this design were cut from an assortment of richly colored and lushly textured fabrics. A good source for these types of scraps are upholstery remnants and secondhand evening dresses.

The sumptuous effect of the fabrics is enhanced by the addition of textured braids and tasseled trim. When gathering together your fabric scraps to make this cushion, don't try to exactly match those used here. Just aim for similar

shades and a wide variety of textures; as the ribbons and braids are so decorative it is better to keep the patch fabrics muted.

LEFT *When choosing seam trims for the cushion, select ones that will stand out visually against the fabric patches. For an alternative colorway see page 89.*
RIGHT *This cushion has the feel of traditional crazy patchwork because of its deep, rich colors and luxurious fabrics.*

MATERIALS FOR THE CUSHION

ABOVE *A selection of the crazy-patch fabrics, braids, ribbons, and other trims used on the cushion cover. The wider the variety of seam trims and fabric patches, the livelier the final crazy-patchwork composition will be.*

You will need

- **Crazy-patch scraps** ~ solid-colored and bicolor brocades and solid-colored velvets and chenilles, all in rich, muted, jewel-like colors
- **Foundation fabric** ~ lightweight fusible woven interfacing
- **Seam decoration** ~ an assortment of narrow metallic and patterned braids, and patterned and tartan ribbons
- **Sewing threads** ~ basting thread, invisible monofilament thread, and matching thread for backing
- **Side borders** ~ piece of brocade fabric at least 16in (40cm) by 14in (35cm)
- **Trimmings** ~ chunky cord with inset seam allowance, metallic braid, and patterned ribbon for border panels, and a length of tasseled fringe for ends of cushion cover
- **Cushion cover back** ~ piece of one of crazy-patch fabrics
- **Pillow form** ~ to fit cushion cover
- **Fasteners** ~ snaps or zipper for cushion cover opening (optional)

MAKING THE CUSHION PATCHWORK

THE CRAZY-PATCHWORK panel on this cushion is a simple square block stitched into the center of the front of the cover. The finished Braided Cushion measures 24in (60cm) by 12in (30cm). A smaller or bigger cover can be made by reducing or enlarging the size of the patch foundation in

Step 1. If desired the patch edges can be machine zigzagged before the trims are stitched in place; this makes the patchwork extra durable. See pages 22 and 26 for more detailed instructions on how to bond patches in place and cover the raw edges of the patches with braids.

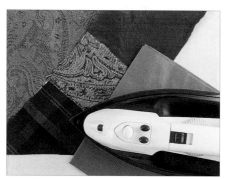

1 Mark the size for the finished crazy-patchwork panel, 12 in (30cm) square, onto the glue side of the fusible interfacing using a water soluble pen. Cut out the square adding an extra ³⁄₄in (2cm) for the seam allowance. Begin arranging the patches in one corner so that they are slightly overlapping and the seam allowance is covered.

2 Once the first few patches have been arranged, fuse them in place. To avoid the iron coming in contact with the glue on the interfacing, place a piece of paper over the exposed interfacing. Continue in this way, positioning a few patches then bonding them in place, until the whole foundation fabric is covered, including the seam allowance.

3 Once all the crazy patches have been bonded to the fusible foundation, use the narrow braids and ribbons to cover the raw edges between the patches. Pin and baste the trims in place using a different braid or ribbon for each side of a patch. Where possible cover the cut ends of the trims with adjacent trims as shown.

4 Set the sewing machine to zigzag stitch and thread it with invisible monofilament thread (see page 22). Stitching down each side of the braids and ribbons, machine zigzag them in place. Once all the trims have been secured with machine stitches, remove the basting threads. Do not trim the edges of the patchwork to straighten them until the remaining embellishments have been added.

5 Cut small tassels from the tasseled fringe (or make your own). Then stitch tassels to some of the corners of the crazy patches; this will help to hide any awkward seam collisions. Finally, trim the edges to size. The patchwork panel should measure about 13¹⁄₂in (34cm) square including the seam allowance.

6 For the border panels on the cushion cover, cut two pieces of brocade each 7½in (19cm) wide and 13½in (34cm) long. Sew one piece to one end of the patchwork, taking a ¾in (2cm) seam allowance. Trim the seam and press open. Using monofilament thread, stitch a length of braid over the seam line between the patchwork panel and the brocade border. Next to the braid topstitch the patterned ribbon and the cord, with the cord seam tape inserted under the edge of the ribbon. Stitch the tasseled trim in place 1in (2.5cm) from the end. Repeat on the other end of the patchwork. Turn to page 122 for instructions on backing the cushion.

Patch corner decorations

Instead of tassels, you could use attractive ribbon rosettes to decorate the corners of the patches on your Braided Cushion. See page 126 for how to make single and double ribbon rosettes.

PATCHWORK ALTERNATIVES

THE COLORS and fabrics shown on page 86 are just guidelines for your version of the Braided Cushion. They are illustrated to give you an idea of what colors will work well together and how to build up a luxurious and rich surface with jewel colors and upholstery-type textures. To some extent your patchwork will depend on what types of scraps you have at hand, but they will also depend on the subtleties of your own personal color taste. If the color scheme given for a project is not what you are looking for, try alternative color combinations until you find one you like. (See pages 16–19.)

RIGHT *The sample shown here is an alternative colorway that could form the basis for your collection of patches instead of the ones on the Braided Cushion. This alternative colorway for the crazy patchwork uses both the right and wrong sides of intricately patterned silk tie fabrics. The arrangement is enhanced by the herringbone stitch worked in gold metallic threads over the patch joins and the metal buttons.*

RIBBON BOX

A sumptuous circular patchwork pieced from silk, satin, and

velvet ribbons covers the top of this round box. Embellished with an array of machine

satin stitches, the design is an elegant medley of color.

THIS ROUND ribbon patchwork was inspired by the fanned patches that were often integrated into the corners or centers of antique crazy-quilt blocks. A variety of machine satin stitches were used to secure the ribbon scraps. If your sewing machine does not have the facility to make these fancy stitches, a simple zigzag and colorful thick twisted threads can be used instead (see page 25 for more about machine embroidery).

The size of your ready-made box is up to you, but one with a loosely fitting lid is essential since the base of the box will be covered with a ribbon patchwork stitched to a foundation fabric.

LEFT *The lavish multicolored tassel and the variegated thread colors on the machine satin stitches soften the regular geometry of these radiating patches. Since piecing the wedge-shaped patches around the circular foundation fabric requires the skill of an experienced patchworker, an easier-to-make but equally elegant ribbon patchwork alternative is given on page 93.*

RIGHT *The Ribbon Box measures 8in (20cm) in diameter and is 3¹/₂in (9cm) deep. Lined with a jewel-colored velvet, this luxurious box with its rainbow of colors would make an excellent container for jewelry or silk scarves.*

MATERIALS FOR THE RIBBON BOX

ABOVE *A selection of the satin, silk, and velvet ribbons in shades of the rainbow, the tassel threads, and the variegated machine embroidery thread used to make the Ribbon Box patchwork cover.*

You will need

- **Crazy-patch scraps** ~ an assortment of ³/₄in (2cm) wide plain satin, silk, and velvet ribbons, in jewel shades
- **Center circle** ~ an extra-wide red satin ribbon or patch for central circle on lid
- **Foundation fabric** ~ strong cotton fabric in white
- **Embroidery thread** ~ variegated machine embroidery thread in complementary tones and colors
- **Box** ~ neutral-colored round cardboard box with lid
- **Lid trim** ~ velvet ribbon same width as depth of box lid
- **Tassel** ~ ready-made tassel or twisted silk or pearl cotton in various colors
- **Sewing threads** ~ basting thread
- **Special tool** ~ hat pin or craft stiletto for piercing box top for tassel
- **Fabric glue** ~ for finishing box

MAKING THE BOX PATCHWORK

Two pieces of crazy patchwork are needed to cover a box: one to cover the base of the box and one to cover the box lid.

For a round box, the circular patchwork for the lid is made large enough to cover only the top of the lid; the lip of the lid is covered with ribbon after the patchwork is glued to the box. (See pages 76–79 for covering a square or rectangular box.)

When piecing the wedge-shaped patches on the circular patchwork, remember to carefully overlap the selvage edge of the patch so that it forms straight line radiating from the marked center point on the foundation fabric. Double check this angle when the patches reach the quarter markings on the foundation, lining up a patch seam line with the marking.

To avoid bulk under the lid, make the patchwork for the base of the box with some of the finer ribbons.

1 Using a water soluble pen, draw on the foundation fabric a rectangle as long as the circumference of the box base plus an extra 1in (2.5cm) for the overlap, and as wide as the exact depth of the box. Cut out the rectangle. Baste ribbons along the length of the foundation, butting the edges together and aligning the selvages of the first and last ribbon with the edge of the foundation. Machine embroider the patch joins with the variegated thread. Then trim away the extra foundation fabric under the first and last ribbons.

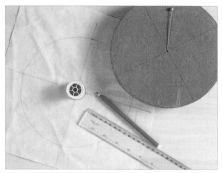

2 Next, begin the patchwork for the top of the lid. Mark the center of the box lid and pierce the center point with a hat pin or craft stiletto. Trace the circular outline of the top of the box lid onto the foundation fabric and mark the center through the hole. Divide the circle into quarters with two perpendicular lines and trace a small circle at the center using a thread spool. Then mark a 3/4in (2cm) seam allowance around the lid outline on the foundation fabric. Cut out the foundation leaving an extra 2in (5cm) outside the seam allowance.

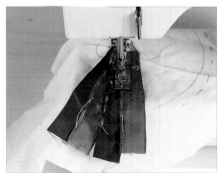

3 Without attaching them to the foundation fabric, baste the first two ribbon patches together so that the second ribbon overlaps the first to form a V-shape. On the wrong side, trim away the excess fabric on the first patch which extends past the basting. Then place the two basted patches in position on the foundation. Stitching through the foundation and leaving the first two patches unattached, baste then machine embroider the next patch in place. Lift up the third patch and trim away the excess ribbon on the second patch. Next, baste the fourth patch in place.

4 Continue piecing the ribbons onto the foundation, machine embroidering one patch in place and trimming the excess ribbon of the previous patch under it before stitching the next patch. When you reach the first patch, slip the free edge of the last patch under it and machine embroider the remaining patch joins. Place the patchwork face down on a padded surface and press. Then redraw the lid circumference on the wrong side of the patchwork. Machine stitch just outside the outline, and stitch a second line 1/4in (6mm) outside the first to secure the patch ends.

5 From the wide red ribbon or patch, cut a circle of fabric large enough to cover the untidy patch ends at the center of the lid patchwork. To correctly position the circle at the center of the crazy patches, push a pin through the patchwork center from the wrong side through to the right side, then push the same pin through the exact center of the red circle. Pin and baste the red circle in place. Using the variegated machine embroidery thread as for the other patches, machine embroider around the raw edge of the circle to cover it and secure the patch in place.

6 Turn the lid patchwork to the wrong side and trim the seam allowance to within ³⁄₄in (2cm) of the lid outline. This allowance will be folded onto the lip of the box lid and glued in place, then covered with a ribbon. Next, place the circular lid patchwork face down on a padded surface and press again with a warm iron. Press the rectangular ribbon patchwork for the box base (made in Step 1) in the same way. If you cannot find a ready-made tassel that suits the color scheme of your box, make a multicolored tassel like the one shown left, using several colors of a thick twisted embroidery thread such as buttonhole silk or pearl cotton. Instructions for making a tassel are given on page 126. Turn to page 125 for how to attach the patchwork and the tassel to the round ready-made box.

PATCHWORK ALTERNATIVES

ALTHOUGH THERE are many possible alternative crazy patchwork designs that would suit a box cover, ribbons are always a good idea for the type of small patches needed for a box. This is because the ribbon selvages provide secure, smooth edges. But the ribbons can be pieced together in an arrangment that is easier to work than the precise V-shapes of the design on the previous pages. For a quicker ribbon crazy patchwork, try a random patch arrangement. Or, simply overlap the ribbons and stitch them together in simple stripe formation.

RIGHT *To make this alternative design, first stitch several small individual patchworks by zigzagging the parallel ribbons onto separate foundations with invisible machine thread. Then piece the separate sections onto a circular foundation, cutting them into pie shapes and lapping the ribbon selvage edge of each patch piece over the cut edge of the adjacent piece.*

BEADED FRAME

This vibrant crazy patchwork is pieced onto a foundation fabric, encrusted

with gold beads, then stretched over a padded frame mount. It provides a suitable

setting for the reproduction of a favorite painting.

SMALL PROJECTS like this frame are ideal for learning how to create interesting interactions between colors, fabric textures, and random geometric shapes. There is plenty of time to play with these design elements, arranging and rearranging crazy patches until the composition contains just the right amount of harmony and contrast. As there is no call for a hardwearing surface, making a frame also allows for the use of precious textile scraps and delicate bead embroidery. For an alternative to the bead embellishment, see page 97.

LEFT *The instructions on the following pages for the Beaded Frame are for a finished size of 8½in (21.5cm) by 9½in (24cm) and an aperture 3½in (9cm) by 5½in (14cm). If this size is not suitable for your chosen picture, simply alter the measurements of the cardboard mount, keeping the frame area wide enough for a generous display of crazy patches.*
RIGHT *The striking contrasts of rich, firey reds, warm greens, cool blues and purples, and glittering gold beads make this design spring to life. In addition, the varied textured weaves and fabric prints lend a wonderfully tactile quality.*

MATERIALS FOR THE FRAME

ABOVE *A selection of the velvet, silk, brocade, plaid, and paisley crazy-patch fabrics and beads used on the Beaded Frame.*

You will need

- **Crazy-patch scraps** ~ velvets, silks, brocades, plaids, and paisleys, in rich reds, blues, purples, and greens
- **Foundation fabric** ~ lightweight fusible woven white interfacing
- **Beads** ~ gold glass and metal bugle and round beads for decorating seams
- **Sewing thread** ~ basting thread, strong gold-colored thread for sewing on beads, and monofilament thread
- **Special equipment** ~ slate frame for stretching patchwork to sew on beads, and craft knife and cutting board for cutting out center of picture mount
- **Picture mount** ~ two pieces of strong cardboard each 8½in (21.5cm) by 9½in (24cm), one for frame and one for backing
- **Padding** ~ thick polyester batting same size as cardboard picture mount
- **Fabric glue** ~ for finishing frame

EVENING BAG

Glittering gold and silver textiles and trims make for the ultimate in

crazy patchwork luxuriousness. If you're looking for an excuse to buy small

remnants of the most sumptuous fabrics in the shop, here it is.

THE BEST PART of this project is searching for the exquisite scraps, buttons, ready-made cutouts, and trims. You can either purchase very small remnants for the patches, or cut swatches from thrift-shop evening wear—shimmering secondhand blouses or boleros are often available at reasonable prices, especially if they are damaged. A wide range of gold and silver braids and buttons can be found in specialty shops, and for unique finishing touches, a few antique buttons and trims from local flea markets can be added to the ensemble.

LEFT *The choice of scraps for the Evening Bag makes a heavily and intricately textured crazy patchwork. Because the fabrics are relatively similar in thickness and are equally luxurious, they blend together successfully. For a less ornate evening bag patchwork, see the silk patch and metallic machine embroidery alternative on page 101.*

RIGHT *Measuring 18in (45cm) deep by 12in (30cm) wide, the finished bag allows ample room for anything you need for an evening out. To adapt the design to a smaller size, select narrower braids, and tiny button and motif trims.*

MATERIALS FOR THE BAG

ABOVE *A selection of the crazy-patch fabrics, appliqué motifs, buttons, and trims used on the Evening Bag.*

You will need

- **Crazy-patch scraps** ~ gold, silver, and black metallic fabrics in solids, brocades, and laces
- **Seam decoration** ~ narrow gold and silver metallic braids and fringes
- **Foundation fabric** ~ lightweight fusible woven white interfacing
- **Appliqué cutouts** ~ ready-made metallic and sequin motifs for decorating center of some patches
- **Buttons** ~ gold and silver buttons or charms for decorating patch corners
- **Lining** ~ piece of dark silk fabric 25in (63cm) by 25in (63cm)
- **Drawstring** ~ 65in (165cm) long gold cord with a tassel at each end
- **Sewing threads** ~ basting thread, invisible monofilament thread, and matching thread for sewing lining
- **Trim** ~ 25in (64cm) of a fringed braid for bottom edge of finished bag

WOOL SCARF

The patches of this warm scarf are pieced directly onto each other

without a foundation fabric. This eliminates the need for a lining and makes the

wrong side of the scarf as soft and colorful as the right side.

THIS SCARF IS MADE almost entirely of wool scraps. Wools are sometimes overlooked as candidates for patch-work since they are more difficult to handle than cottons. But it is a shame to pass up those rich wool colors. The special technique used to piece this scarf is called a "lapped" seam; the patches are overlapped and the raw edges secured on both the right and wrong sides with invisible thread.

ABOVE *The scarf patches are stitched together into rectangles, then these blocks are joined to make a long strip. Simple stitches in sharp shades of crewel wool decorate the patch edges. The finished scarf is 17¹/₄in (44cm) wide by 67in (170cm) long.*
RIGHT *Optional extras for the scarf are scraps of secondhand embroideries. The instructions for making the original cross-stitch flowers in the center of the picture are given on page 104.*

MATERIALS FOR THE SCARF

RIGHT *A selection of the crazy-patch fabric scraps and crewel wool embroidery yarn used on the Wool Scarf.*

You will need

- **Crazy-patch scraps** ~ reversible wools tartan, tweed, solid-colored, and paisley fabrics, all in rich antique colors (see sample fabrics, left, and photographs of scarf for color ideas)
- **Embroidered scraps** ~ two or three scraps of secondhand fabric with hand embroidery (optional)
- **Embroidery thread** ~ crewel wool yarn in an assortment of complementary colors for motifs, seam decoration, and scarf edging and fringe
- **Waste canvas** ~ 11-stitches-to-the-inch (2.5cm) waste canvas for cross-stitch embroidery on wool fabric (optional)
- **Sewing threads** ~ basting thread and invisible monofilament thread
- **Special tool** ~ crochet hook or latch-hook for scarf fringe

MAKING THE SCARF PATCHWORK

T̲HE SCARF IS made up of seven rectangular sections of crazy patchwork. Each section is made separately and the blocks are only joined together after all the patch seams are embroidered. Note that most of the patches are 10in (26cm) long randomly shaped wedge-like strips. For variety, or if your scraps are small, the strips can be pieced into the correct length before the strips are joined to make the individual rectangular section (see Step 2).

1 Before beginning the patchwork, if desired work cross-stitch motifs on one or more patches using waste canvas (see page 28). Use your own cross-stitch designs or the one shown here, which is given on page 115.

2 Piece the first piece of crazy patchwork into a rectangle 10in (26cm) by 18in (46cm). To do this first cut the patches into 11in (28cm) long wedge-shaped strips as shown above, then and baste them together so that they overlap exactly ³/₈in (1cm) at the joins. Once the patches are basted together, machine zigzag (see page 22) the raw edges on *both* sides of the patchwork using invisible monofilament thread. (If some of your scraps are too short to form a long wedge, then overlap, baste, and zigzag them together before beginning to piece the rectangle.) Measuring the patchwork pieces as they are joined, make six more rectangular blocks in the same way, but varying the wedge shapes and fabrics from section to section. Trim the edges to straighten them if necessary.

3 Next, decorate the joins between the patches with hand embroidery. Changing the color used and the stitch used on each line of stitching and using four strands of crewel wool, work cross, herringbone, vandyke, blanket, or wheatear stitch over the patch overlaps (see pages 109–111). Work the embroidery so that it is as wide as the overlaps and so that it is as neat as possible on the wrong side (see right).

4 Baste and machine zigzag the seven finished patchwork pieces together, joining along the long edges and overlapping the raw edges $^3/_8$in (1cm) as for the patches. The scarf now measures 18in (46cm) by about 67$^3/_4$in (176cm). Cover the new joins with hand embroidery, again using four strands of crewel wool. Trim the edges if necessary.

5 Turn $^3/_8$in (1cm) to the wrong side around the scarf edge and baste. Using four strands of crewel wool, work hand embroidery over the basted edge, changing the color of thread after each needlefull is used up. If desired, work closed buttonhole stitch as shown here, or another buttonhole or blanket stitch variation (see page 109).

6 To make the fringe at the ends of the scarf, for each fringe tassel cut about sixteen 6in (15cm) lengths of crewel wool and fold them in half to form a loop. Insert a crochet hook under the buttonhole stitch, and pull the loop through. Pull the yarn ends through the loop and tighten. Change the yarn color with each tassel along the fringe.

PATCHWORK ALTERNATIVES

THE MOST IMPORTANT thing to consider when looking for alternative patchwork ideas for scarves, is whether the finished piece will be comfortable to wear. Fine wools stitched together without a foundation fabric or lining are, of course, an excellent choice as they are warm, soft, and drape well. So an excellent alternative for the design on page 102 would be fine wool crepes in bright solid colors. For an evening scarf, antique or modern lace would be a good choice.

RIGHT *Quicker to make than the Wool Scarf, this lace version has a panel of patchwork stitched to each end of a long, wide strip of lace net. To make the lace patchwork, machine zigzag the lace patches to a net foundation. Then zigzag narrow lace braids over the patch edges. Turn the side edges of the patches and net to the inside and machine stitch. Join the panels to the scarf ends by sandwiching the edges between satin ribbons. Finish the scarf ends with satin ribbons, lace braid, and ready-made fringe.*

STITCH
GLOSSARY

Embroidery gives crazy patchwork its unique charm. The stitches used are usually simple ones, and the rich appearance comes merely from the variety of decorations.

EVEN MOST BEGINNER embroiderers will already have mastered many of the stitches given in the stitch glossary. The step-by-step instructions are included to serve as a reminder of how the basic stitches are worked and to introduce a few stitches that are less familiar but just as simple to master.

Although any number of embroidery stitches could be used on crazy patchworks, those that follow are all that is needed to work eye-catching motifs (see pages 28 and 29), attractive letters and numerals (see pages 32–35), simple edgings for appliquéd shapes (see pages 30 and 31), and lavish seam embellishments (see pages 24 and 25). The sampler pictured on the right features almost all of the stitches included in the step-by-step stitch illustrations.

The embroidery stitches are followed by charts and outlines for embroidered letters, numerals, and motifs that can be used in the projects.

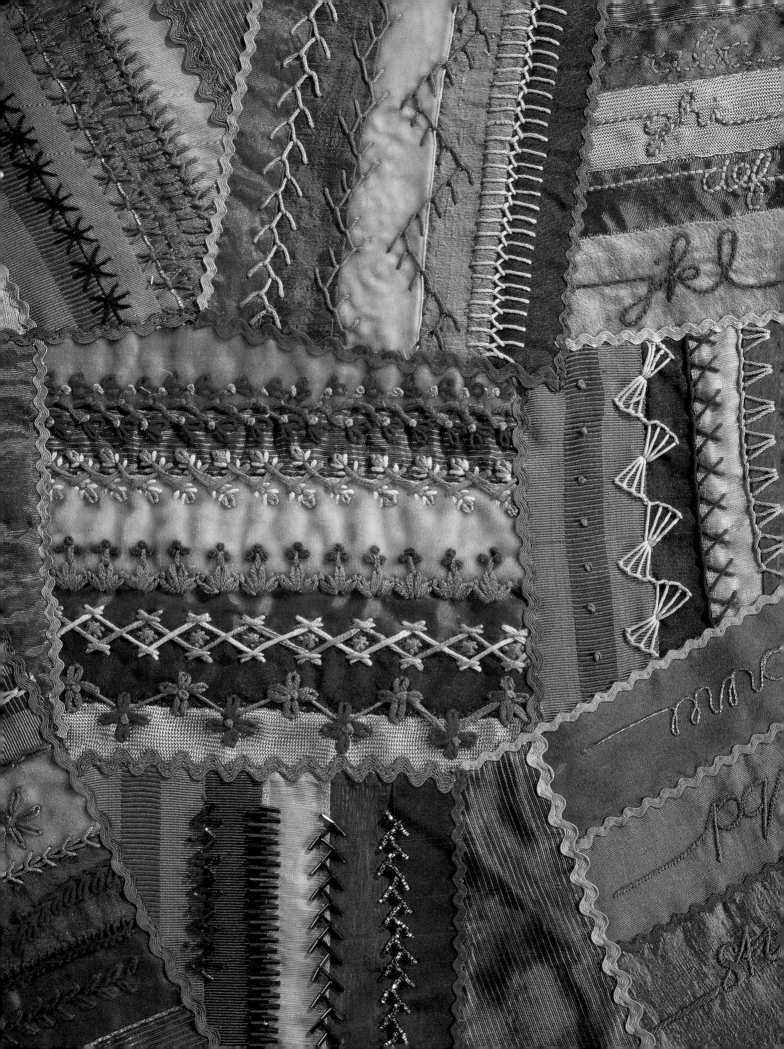

CHAIN STITCH & LAZY DAISY STITCH

WHEN WORKED individually instead of in a continuous linked line, chain stitches are called either detached chain or lazy daisy stitch.

 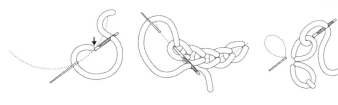 

CABLE CHAIN STITCH

WHEN THIS knotted stitch is worked, the needle is twisted around the thread before and after each elongated chain is formed.

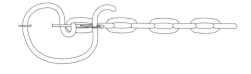 

WHEATEAR STITCH

AFTER THE two straight arms of this stitch are worked, the needle is passed behind them without piercing the fabric to form a loop.

PETAL STITCH

PETAL STITCH is a clever combination of lazy daisy stitch and stem stitch. It is most effective when worked in curved or wavy lines.

VANDYKE STITCH

THE LOOPS of this stitch are linked together without the needle piercing the fabric. It forms an impressive and unusual seam decoration.

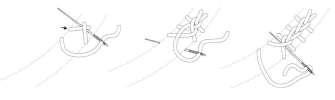 

FEATHERED CHAIN STITCH

WHEN WORKED with a thick twisted thread, feathered chain stitch forms a wide, distinctive zigzag ideal for decorating crazy-patch seams.

FEATHER STITCH & DOUBLE FEATHER STITCH

FEATHER STITCH and the more elaborate double feather stitch, which forms a wide zigzag, are both commonly found on antique crazy quilts.

OPEN CRETAN STITCH & CRETAN STITCH

CRETAN STITCH is worked in exactly the same way as open cretan stitch, except that the stitches are longer and spaced closer together.

 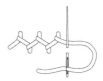 

FRENCH KNOT

A VERY effective, raised stitch, a French knot has the appearance of a little bead. It is often used to embellish other stitches.

STRAIGHT STITCH & SHEAF STITCH

STRAIGHT STITCH can be worked in any length, on its own or in combination with other stitches. If forms the base for the "tied" sheaf stitch.

STAR STITCH

STAR STITCH can be formed with only two equal-sized cross-stitches, or with the addition of a third, smaller cross-stitch tying the center.

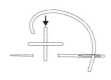  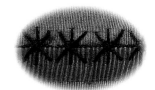

HERRINGBONE STITCH VARIATIONS

HERRINGBONE STITCH is worked spaced apart and the close version close together. The laced version has a second thread laced through it.

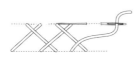 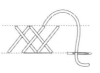 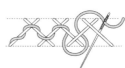 

ALPHABETS AND MOTIFS

The following motifs, alphabets, and numerals are those used for the crazy-

patchwork projects. The cross-stitch designs should be worked stitch-by-stitch from the charts

and the other motifs traced and transferred onto the fabric patches.

THE CHARTED cross-stitch motifs, letters, and numerals given below, opposite, and on page 116 can be worked onto any evenweave fabric (such as aida), or onto non-evenweave with the aid of waste canvas (see page 29 for more about working cross-stitch over waste canvas). The finished size of the cross-stitch designs depend on the size of the aida squares or the number of threads or fabric squares each stitch is worked over.

The linear illustrations of letters, numerals, and motifs on pages 117–119 are for satin stitch (and beaded) dates and messages, gilded motifs, a sewing-pattern piece, appliqué cutouts, and linear motifs. Unless otherwise stated, these designs are shown actual size (see page 28 for transferring techniques). Some of the motifs (and the pattern piece) are too large to provide full size, and have had to be included in the Stitch Glossary smaller than actual size. These reduced illustrations can be enlarged on a photocopier; specific enlargement percentages are given with the illustrations.

CROSS-STITCH ALPHABET AND NUMERALS *Use the alphabet and numerals below to work the cross-stitch words (or dates) onto evenweave aida fabric for the Baby Quilt on pages 60–63.*

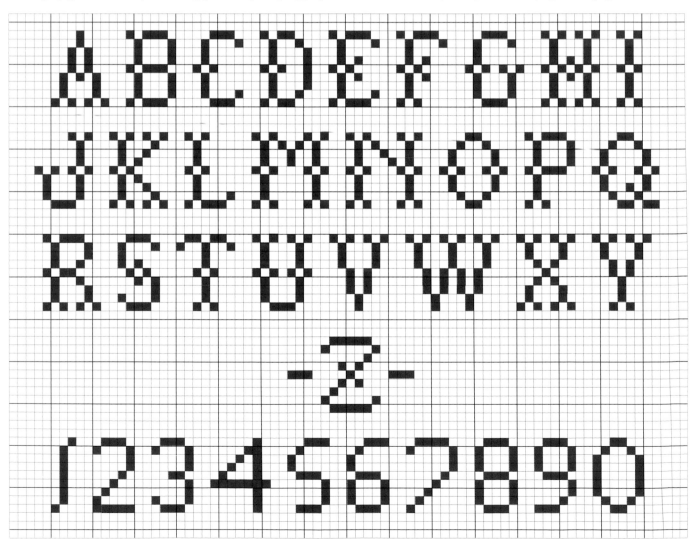

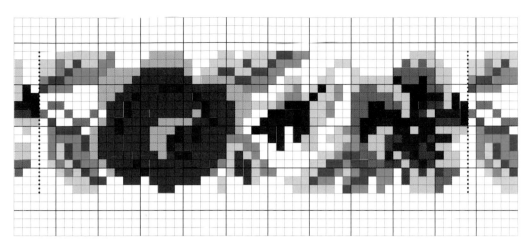

CROSS-STITCH FLOWERS

Use the motif on the left to work the floral cross-stitch embroidery over waste canvas onto a wool patch for the Wool Scarf on pages 102–105. Work the motif and repeat (between the dotted lines) as many times as desired along the strip of fabric.

COLOR KEY

- Brown
- Lime
- Mid-green
- Dark green
- Lilac
- Mauve
- Taupe
- Pink
- Cerise
- Red
- Burgundy
- Yellow

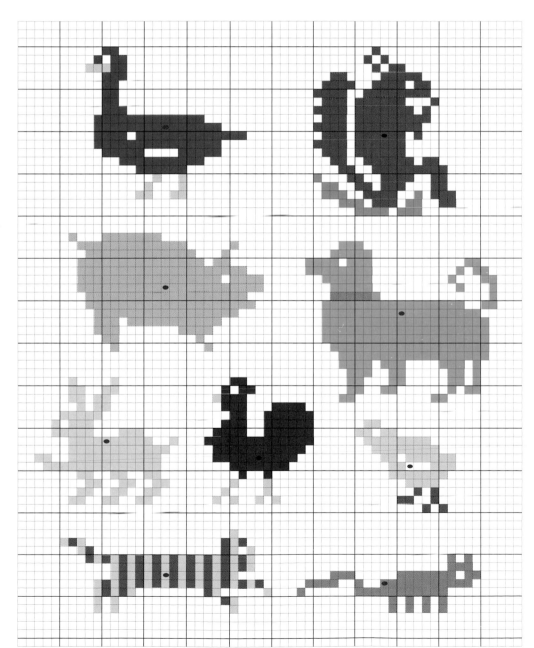

CROSS-STITCH ANIMALS

Use the motifs on the left to work the cross-stitch animals onto evenweave aida fabric patches for the Cross-stitch Baby Quilt on pages 60–63. Begin working each motif at the marked center.

COLOR KEY

- Rust
- Lime
- Mid-green
- Aqua
- Blue
- Mid-pink
- Pink
- Red
- Yellow

MONOCHROME CROSS-STITCH MOTIFS *Use the motifs above to work the cross-stitch embroidery over waste canvas onto cotton fabric patches for the Cross-stitch Cushion on pages 38–41. Begin working each motif at the marked center.*

A B C D E F G H I
J K L M N O P Q R
S T U V W X Y Z &

1 2 3 4 5 6 7 8 9 0

SATIN STITCH ALPHABET AND NUMERALS *Use the alphabet and numerals above for the satin stitch monogram on the Gilded Picture on pages 64–67 and for the pinned and beaded date and letters on the Beaded Heart on pages 72–75.*

GILDED APPLIQUÉ MOTIFS *Use the illustrations below and on the left for the motifs on the Gilded Picture on pages 64–67.*

LAUNDRY BAG BACKSTITCH

MOTIFS *Use the illustrations above for the backstitch motifs on the Embroidered Laundry Bag on pages 46–49. For the correct motif sizes, enlarge those shown here to 142%.*

STUFFED HEART PATTERN PIECE
*Use this heart shape to make the felt heart for the Gingham
Heart on pages 50–53 and the Beaded Heart on pages 72–75,
and for the backing on the hearts. For the correct heart
template size, enlarge the shape shown here to 200%.*

CHILD'S PICTURE EMBROIDERY MOTIFS
*To use the motifs above for the picture on page 67,
enlarge to 142%. Work the lines in backstitch, the
cat's paw pads and the flower centers in French
knots, and the flowers in lazy daisy stitches.*

APPLIQUÉ HEART, STAR, AND FLOWER
*Use the motifs below for the appliqué on the heart
on page 51. The flower shape shows the backstitch
lines; cut out slightly outside the backstitch.*

TOY BAG BACKSTITCH MOTIFS
*Use the motifs above and to the left for the
toy bag on page 50. Work all the lines in
backstitch. Then using a contrasting color, lace
the backstitch on the jumping rope rings and
the teddy's bow to form whipped backstitch
(see page 108 for whipped backstitch).*

FINISHING TECHNIQUES

The following pages contain detailed instructions for completing your crazy patchwork projects and for making a stuffed heart before decorating it with patches.

Most of the projects in the book are begun with the preparation of a piece of crazy patchwork. The instructions accompanying the individual designs explain how to stitch the desired embroidery or appliqué onto the scraps, how to piece the patches onto the foundation fabric, and how to add the seam embellishments. (They also offer alternative patchwork design ideas.)

The directions in this chapter show how to turn the completed crazy patchwork piece into the cushion, picture, bag, or quilt it was intended for, or how to use it to cover a box, lampshade, or frame. There are also step-by-step instructions for how to make the stuffed heart-shaped base for the two sumptuous keepsake hearts.

On the last page of this chapter are directions for making tassels and ribbon rosettes. These finishing touches are useful and attractive embellishments for crazy-patchwork designs and both can be stitched to patch corners to hide awkward joins on braid or ribbon seam decoration.

CRAZY-PATCHWORK FRAMES

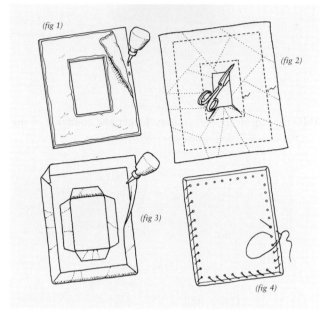

CRAZY-PATCHWORK TRIMS

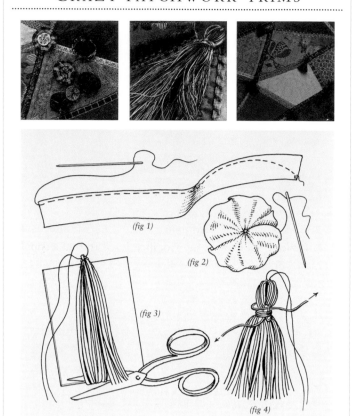

Covering a frame

THESE INSTRUCTIONS are for finishing the *Beaded Frame* on pages 94–97, but you can also use them to complete your own crazy-patchwork frame cover.

Make the crazy patchwork to fit the cardboard frame. If necessary, lightly press the finished patchwork on the wrong side over a padded surface.

Next, cut the piece of polyester batting to the same size as the cardboard frame *(fig 1)*. Glue the batting to the front of the frame and allow the glue to dry before proceeding.

Then machine stitch the inner and outer frame outlines onto the crazy-patchwork piece; position the stitching lines slightly outside the outlines so that they will align with the edges of the cardboard when the fabric edges are glued to the back of the frame. Cut out the fabric inside the frame aperture area 1in (2.5cm) from the outline. Clip the fabric diagonally into the aperture corners, but do not cut through the machine stitching *(fig 2)*.

Lay the prepared patchwork on top of the padded side of the frame. Turn the frame over, pull the fabric edges to the back of the frame, and glue them in place *(fig 3)*. Allow the glue to dry before proceeding.

Next, attach the remaining piece of cardboard to the back of the frame. Either glue the cardboard in place, or punch holes around the edge and stitch it to the fabric around the edge of the frame, using a strong thread *(fig 4)*.

Making a ribbon rosette

RIBBON ROSSETTES can be used to decorate patch corners or to tie padded quilts (see pages 89 and 124). The length of the ribbon used for a rosette depends on the ribbon width—about 4¹⁄₂in (11.5cm) for a ¹⁄₂in (12mm) wide ribbon, more for a wider ribbon, and less for a narrower one. (If in doubt, cut the ribbon only after gathering it.) Beginning with a couple backstitches to secure the thread at the corner of the ribbon end, work a small running stitch, curving up to the opposite edge and work along this edge to the end *(fig 1)*. Then pull the ribbon to gather it *(fig 2)*, maneuvering the ribbon ends to the wrong side. Secure the thread at the back and leave a long end for stitching in place. For a double rosette, gather a narrow ribbon and a wide ribbon together.

Making a tassel

INSTEAD OF purchasing expensive ready-made tassels for crazy-patchwork projects, make your own using thick embroidery threads. Cut a piece of cardboard to the desired length of the tassel, and wrap a generous amount of thread around it. Next, wrap a length of thread a few times around the strands at one end of the cardboard, and knot, leaving long loose ends for stitching the tassel in place; then cut the strands at the other end of the tassel *(fig 3)*. Wrap another length of thread around the top of the tassel, linking and securing the ends under the wrapping as shown *(fig 4)*.

BIBLIOGRAPHY

History

ATKINS, Jaqueline, *Shared Threads, Quilting Together Past and Present*, Viking Studio Books, New York, 1994.

BISHOP, Robert, *see Safford*.

FOX, Sandi, *Wrapped in Glory*, Los Angeles County Museum of Art and Thames and Hudson, New York, 1990.

LAVITT, Wendy, *see Weissman*.

SAFFORD, Carleton L, and Robert Bishop, *America's Quilts and Coverlets*, E P Dutton and Co, Inc, New York, 1972, and Cassell and Collier McMillan, London, 1974.

WEISSMAN, Judith Reiter and Wendy Lavitt, *Labors of Love, America's Textiles and Needlework 1650–1930*, Knopf, New York, 1987.

Information

COLBY, Averil, *Patchwork*, Batsford, London, 1958.

MONTANO, Judith, *The Crazy Quilt Handbook*, C & T Publishing, Lafayette, California, 1986.

———, *Elegant Stitches*, C & T Publishing, Lafayette, California, 1995.

Inspiration

LEBOUX, Caroline, *Fabrics, The Decorative Art of Textiles*, Clarkson N Potter Inc, New York, 1994.

QUARTERMAIN, Carolyn, *Unwrapped*, Conran Octopus, London, 1997.

PHOTOGRAPHY CREDITS

All of the photographs in the book, except for those in the introduction, were shot by John Heseltine. The publishers would like to thank the following for the photographs in the introduction:

Pages 6 and *7*, Embroiderers' Guild; *page 8*, Janet Haigh; *page 9*, Jonathan Keenan.

SUPPLIERS' CREDITS

The author would like to thank Jim Moeller at The Silver Thimble for all his support and for supplying the Au Ver a Soie silk yarns used in the projects, Bogod Sewing Machines in London for the loan of a Bernina sewing machine, DMC for supplying cotton and wool embroidery threads and counted-thread fabrics, and Cara Ackerman at DMC for her unfailing efficiency.

DMC addresses

To find a supplier of DMC threads near you, contact one of the distributors listed below for information:

U.K.: DMC Creative World Ltd, Pullman Road, Wigston, Leicestershire LE18 2DY, England. Tel: (0116) 281 1040. Fax: (0116) 281 3592.

U.S.A.: DMC Corporation, Building 10, Port Kearny, South Kearny, New Jersey 07032. Tel: (201) 589 0606. Fax: (201) 589 8931.

Canada: As for U.S.A.

Australia: DMC Needlecraft Pty Ltd, 51-66 Carrington Road, Marrickville, NSW 2204 or PO Box 317, Earlswood, NSW 2206. Tel: (02) 559 3088. Fax: (02) 559 5338.

Au Ver a Soie addresses

Au Ver a Soie produce silk embroidery threads that can be used for working crazy patchwork embroidery. To find a supplier of Au Ver a Soie threads near you, contact one of the distributors listed below for information:

U.K.: The Silver Thimble, The Old Malthouse, Clarence Street, Bath BA1 5NS, England. Tel: (01225) 423 457. Fax: (01225) 480 448.

U.S.A.: Access Commodities Inc, PO Box 1355, 1129 S. Virginia Street, Terrell, Texas 75160. Tel: (972) 563 3313.

Canada: As for U.S.A.

Australia: Stadia Trading Pty Ltd, Beaconsfield, NSW 2014. Tel: 9565 4666.

ACKNOWLEDGMENTS

Working on this book was a really enjoyable experience, due mainly to the following team of editors and designers whose professional expertise was matched by their great good humor. I would like to thank:

Susan Berry, who personally persuaded me that writing another book was a good idea and who put together the editorial team who helped me to realize my design ideas in such a stimulating environment.

Hilary Jagger, the co-maker of my projects, whose wit and personal taste added much to the breadth of the book's range and who ultimately stopped me from beading the rickrack, disproving the old adage "never work with friends."

Debbie Mole, the art editor, who through her visual empathy with my work, her personal vision of the book, and her sheer hard work and determination has made this book look "summat-like."

Sally Harding, the editor, who—if "God is in the detail"—is destined for sainthood for initiating me into the mysteries of the "step-by-steps" and making sense of my garbled instructions.

John Heseltine, the photographer, who made the patchworks look so sumptuous.

Also, my new-found agent Doreen Montgomery and Mary Jenkins for introducing us.

Wendy and Roy Davies who commissioned my first crazy patchwork portrait.

Lastly, Stephen Jacobson, my husband, for his customary patience when dealing with me, especially while teaching me to "interface with the new technology."

INDEX